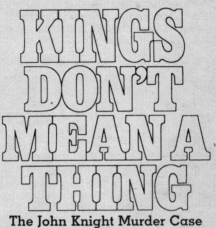

KINGS DON'T MEAN A THING

The John Knight Murder Case

ARTHUR BELL

A BERKLEY BOOK
published by
BERKLEY PUBLISHING CORPORATION

This Berkley book contains the complete
text of the original hardcover edition.
It has been completely reset in a type face
designed for easy reading, and was printed
from new film.

KINGS DON'T MEAN A THING

A Berkley Book / published by arrangement with
William Morrow and Company, Inc.

PRINTING HISTORY
William Morrow edition published 1978
Berkley edition / December 1979

ISBN: 0-425-04212-X

A BERKLEY BOOK® TM 757,375
Berkley Books are published by Berkley Publishing Corporation,
200 Madison Avenue, New York, New York, 10016.
PRINTED IN THE UNITED STATES OF AMERICA

TO ARTHUR EVANS

Contents

THE

KILLING

FLASHBACK, THREE MONTHS. A man parks his car on Twenty-first Street near the Dorchester and waddles toward Spruce—woozy, been drinking since noon. He is humming "Brazil." It is always "Brazil." Not the Aurora Miranda "Brazil," but the Ritchie Family's. "We stood beneath an amber mo-o-on."

As usual, near midnight, the activity has just begun on the street. The man warily surveys the new autumn crop. Tanktops of summer have been replaced with checkered shirts and work boots. Young men decked out as construction workers who have never seen a crane. It used to be glitter. Glitter and be gay. Now it's swagger and be butch. Beneath that pierced ear, behind that strut, lies the soul of a hairdresser, he thinks. These are not his kind of men. None of this is him.

Need another drink. He wanders past the stoops and the lighted delis, heading toward Fifteenth Street, hustlers' row. The sweater he wears is wool, loose-fitting, hand-knit in the Hebrides: pants slightly baggy,

3

disguising the slight paunch that occupies his mind too frequently nowadays. Some poor undiscerning schnook —a pseudo construction worker with myopic vision— might take John Knight for an out-of-town rube. Passable, slightly tipsy, somewhat rugged, no prize.

Doesn't matter. Eye-play games with carefully turned out woodsmen—not for him. Waste of time.

Near the Great Scot Market at Eighteenth Street, something happens to his equilibrium. His legs aren't right. He stumbles, stops, leans against a wrought-iron banister, closes his eyes, inhales several times, flops on the pavement, and knots his legs into a lotus position.

Curious, this gay scene in Philadelphia. This area: a little city unto itself, unlike anything in Detroit, where he had lived and worked for four years, or Boston, where he went to school. A community here. A community without the sanction of law, where gay men are still not legally protected in their jobs. A cop could enter any of the clubs at any time and make multiple arrests, perhaps even arrest someone like him on the street for what is merely on his mind. Interesting that those with careers and reputations to lose flaunt their foolishness while the city sleeps.

But he is different. Swings both ways. Certainly, absolutely, not one of them. Dabbling in perversity, playing tic-tac-toe in the nether world is one thing. Being like them is something he would never admit to himself.

"Are you all right?" asks a Paul Bunyan dress-alike.

John Knight opens his eyes. He nods his head. The inquisitor stands close, puts his arm to Knight's elbow but is shrugged away.

"I'm okay," he answers.

"Just being friendly," says the stranger.

"I'm all right. Just need another drink."

Down Spruce. More of them. A parade. Who are they? Where do they come from? Near the Warwick Hotel, he cuts off a side street and enters the 247 Bar. Cowboys, leathermen, telephone repairmen, ditch-diggers—only by night. By day, copywriters, space salesmen, bookkeepers, shoe clerks.

"Scotch, straight."

He downs it.

"Another."

Small talk with a gas station jockey from Scranton. No, he hasn't seen Gwen Verdon in *Chicago*. Yes, this place is boring. No, I'm not from Philly. Yes, I live alone. Yes, I dig everything. Sorry, I'm not interested, but can I buy you a drink?

The gas station jockey thanks him politely and moves down the bar to sulk in his Rheingold.

Knight orders a double.

"You've had too much," says the bartender.

Knight leaves the change on the counter and splits.

At Fifteenth and Spruce, lined up like cloned derivations of Joan Blondell in a Busby Berkeley production number, are several boys, most of them young, some of them pretty, if you can see through the acne. They are the youths of the evening and the Warner brothers would turn over in their graves.

A few of those on display work as messengers during the day, but most are unemployed, from foster homes, juvenile delinquents, runaways, kids who have nowhere to go and can risk the chance of a beating or a night in jail or an act of love above and beyond the call of genuine passion. Doesn't matter: Omaha, Miami or Milan. A street hustler is ever alert for the big kill, searching for the john who'll set him up in splendor and take him away from "the life."

He eyes the chorus line. He says hello to one of the

kids whom he had once tricked with. The kid breaks from his frozen-pose position, smiles, his teeth in need of a good orthodontist.

"What's up?" the kid asks.

"I'm horny as hell," Knight replies.

The kid stares at Knight's lower lip and suggests they go somewhere. Knight rejects the idea.

"I've got a friend," says the kid. "Someone new to the street. I can fix you up with him, and if it works you pay me thirty dollars. Pay nothing to him. If it doesn't, pay me ten dollars. No hassle."

"Sounds good."

Slowly, the two men walk the four blocks, past the Allegro, where the established Philadelphia homosexual carouses, past Roscoe's, where the liberated homosexual adjourns after his gay activist meeting. They stop at the Hasty-Tasty Deli. Signs on the outside window announce a gay dance, a dog lost, a roommate wanted. Inside, the cashier and grocery clerk talk in "get you, honey" lingo. The customers are friendly and the place is brightly lighted. People can actually see what they're eating—and each other.

The kid sees his friend at the rear table.

"Felix," he says. "This is John."

Felix offers his hand. It is a long hand and he drops it into John's the way a haberdasher would slip a tie into a gift box.

John sits down. He asks Felix if he'd like another coffee. He orders three.

Felix is quiet, the kid chatty, John sulky.

Felix whispers, "Is this guy drunk?"

The kid replies, "No, he's high, he's usually that way." He turns to John. "Do you like Felix?"

John nods.

"So it's a deal?"

"It's a deal. Here."

John pulls a couple of twenties from his pocket and asks the kid to take care of all the negotiations and keep the change.

Five minutes later, a sullen Felix Melendez and an impatient John Knight leave Hasty-Tasty for Knight's $1050-a-month apartment on Rittenhouse Square.

If we are to believe what Felix Melendez later told the kid, "Nothing happened. We smoked a joint, then that guy John fell asleep. I stayed the night and he cooked me breakfast."

Early on the morning of December 11, 1975, the telephone rings at the house where I'm staying in Provincetown. I've asked my New York answering service to be cautious about routing the Provincetown number, to give it out only in case of emergency.

The call is from Tom Morgan, editor in chief of the *Village Voice*. No apologies, no how-are-yous. Straightaway, he asks, "Have you been following this John Knight business?" I don't know what he's talking about. After all, I'm on vacation, enjoying the off-season quiet of P'town, walking the sandy beaches, retiring early, and who the hell is John Knight? I tell Morgan that I haven't seen a paper or heard a radio since leaving New York.

"Never mind," he says. "In a nutshell, the heir to the largest newspaper chain in the country got himself killed on Sunday. It looks like a homosexual thing, perhaps a ritualistic killing. It's got all the earmarks of a great story: money, power, the works. They haven't caught the killer yet. Can you get your ass on a plane to Philadelphia and check it out?"

I hem and haw. On vacation. Don't know a thing about John Knight. Don't know Philadelphia. But Morgan is a con man with an irresistible manner. His method is to tell you how good you are, that you are the only one who can handle the story. He's done it to me before. I've seen him do it to others. Flattery works on writers. And this writer doesn't ordinarily ponder whether that flattery is false or sincere. So Morgan and I get down to terms. He offers double what I usually get for a *Voice* feature, but considerably less than I'd earn from *Esquire*. He also says he'll give me as much space as I need: up to 10,000 words. He suggests I stay in Philadelphia for as long as I have to, "but keep expenses down."

"And keep quiet," he warns. "We don't want the *Times* down there scooping us."

Two hours later, I'm on one of those six-passenger shuttle jobs, flying south of the Provincetown sunset, and by 9 P.M. I'm in the City of Brotherly Love, where the streets are painted red, white and blue in preparation for the Bicentennial, and the closest thing to beach and sand is a poster at the Eastern Airlines terminal advertising a winter vacation in Miami.

Philadelphia. Former home of Princess Grace. Site of the Cary Grant, Katharine Hepburn, James Stewart comedy. Mayor Rizzo. The Philadelphia Flyers. The Liberty Bell. Marian Anderson, Joseph Kallinger, and Kraft cheese. The town that rolls up its lawns at 6 P.M. and closes shop on Sundays.

I check into the Warwick Hotel, a sedate hostelry two blocks from the Dorchester apartment where Knight lived and died. Room service brings up a Jack Daniel's, a ham and cheese on rye, plus the latest *Inquirer*, *Bulletin*, and *News*. As expected, Knight's demise is emblazoned on the front pages. Each of the dailies has an exclusive story. The *News*, where he worked as an editor, plays up the "regular Joe" angle. Paul Janensch, Knight's managing editor, is quoted as saying, "He loved the newspaper business and all aspects

of it. . . . He was a hardworking guy who took instructions well."

Murder victims are usually painted as saints and one
reads the gushy post mortem prose with a certain
amount of cynicism. Yet there seems to be a holding
back in the copy: as if the papers are trying to soft-pedal
Knight's homosexuality, as if they don't want to deal
with it unless they are forced to, as if it isn't kosher to
bring someone out of the closet after death, especially if
that someone happens to be a budding Citizen Kane.
But between the lines are hints that Knight's gayness
was the key to his murder. Allusions to a "secret life," a
search through Philadelphia's underground for possible
suspects, run through the reports.

Having digested the papers, I leave the hotel, hail a
cab, and journey to police headquarters.

Christmas is just around the corner. At Homicide,
holiday tackiness covers the walls. A blue Christmas tree
with silver bulbs, silver tinsel and angel's hair stands
next to an American flag, and next to that stands Inspector Joseph Golden, chief detective on the Knight
case. My timing is perfect. Golden is just about to announce the identity of the Knight killers at a press conference. I'm ushered into a room where perhaps a dozen
reporters wait at the ready. Golden solemnly nods at the
group and places himself behind a desk. A potted poin-
settia droops directly over his head. He looks like a
bruised angel with a scarlet halo.

A fellow officer begins the conference by passing
photographs of the three suspects to each of the
newsmen. "Just a few minutes ago," Golden says, "we
obtained warrants charging each of these persons with
murder, three counts of robbery, attempted murder,
aggravated assault and criminal conspiracy. The
warrants are based on evidence obtained during the

police investigation." Golden describes each of the suspects. His information is sparse:

Felix Melendez, age 19, 5'9", 135 pounds, slender build, green eyes, shoulder-length hair, light complexion, birthmark on the outer right thigh and scar on abdomen.

Salvatore Soli, age 37, 5'4", 128 pounds, slender build, brown eyes, dark brown hair, dark complexion, track marks on both arms, tattoos on right forearm of two hearts and a dove and the words "Mom and Dad." Tattoos on the left upper arms of a cross, a heart and a rose.

Steven Maleno, age 25, 5'9", slender, muscular, dark hair, olive complexion, track marks, married.

Golden maintains that robbery was the motive in the case. He doesn't comment on whether the men are involved in drug traffic or had homosexual involvements. Nor does he talk about a relationship between any of the men and John Knight. "All three are dangerous," he admits. "All three come from South Philadelphia."

It is late. It's been a long day. It is like Provincetown has never happened. I return to the Warwick and sleep.

The phone call that gets me out of bed on Friday, December 12, comes from Dennis Rubini, who teaches a course in alternate life-styles at a Philadelphia university. Rubini has been president of Philadelphia's Gay Activist Alliance and is active in a sadomasochistic "consciousness-raising" group. He asks if I have seen the morning papers. One of the suspects, he reports, has surrendered. He doesn't know which one.

"I hope the cops will stop hassling us now," Dennis grumbles—"us" meaning the homosexual population of Philadelphia.

Rubini goes on to complain that he himself was

picked up by the police because he resembled a sketch of one of the wanted men.

"They took me to Homicide. One of the detectives noticed a bulge in my pocket and thought it might be a gun. Instead, he found a copy of Larry Townsend's *The Leatherman's Handbook*, a manual on sadism and masochism. The officer said, 'Oh, my daughter's interested in leather handiwork, too,' and handed the book back to me.

"Then the cops fingerprinted me, photographed me, and submitted me to a polygraph test. They wanted to know if I had ever engaged in 'abnormal sex.'

"I asked them what they meant by 'abnormal sex.' I said, 'My definition of abnormal or society's definition?' They were stumped. They let it fly. Anyway, I passed the polygraph and they very politely thanked me for my time and trouble."

I make arrangements to see Rubini that night and head toward the Dorchester.

In light of the Knight murder, you'd think they'd have doberman pinschers blockading the establishment. Wrong thought. The Dorchester's doorman politely opens the front door. No questions about identification or inquiries as to who I want to see. The elevators are self-service and, for the hell of it, I ride to the nineteenth floor, where a cop stands vigil outside John Knight's apartment. I show him my New York City Police Department press pass and ask if I can look around. He refuses, as expected, but at least he's polite.

Downstairs in the rental office, the woman in charge admits that the Dorchester has been in a state of frenzy since that nice Mr. Knight was killed. The older residents are buying Fox locks for their doors, she says, and some of them have discussed breaking their leases.

Did Mr. Knight entertain suspicious-looking visitors, I ask?

"Definitely not," she replies. "Mr. Knight was always polite and a gentleman, as were the people he associated with."

Did she recognize any of these faces?

I pull out the wanted pamphlet.

"This one is very familiar," she says, pointing to the mug shot of Felix Melendez.

A moment later, the postman enters the rental office and the woman in charge asks him if he recognizes any of the faces.

"I've seen this fellow here a couple of times with Mr. Knight," he replies, indicating Melendez. "Isn't he the fellow who surrendered?"

"I don't know," shrugs the woman. "I just work here."

The man who surrendered wasn't Felix Melendez. It was Steven Maleno. Five hours after Inspector Golden had released the suspect's name to the press, Maleno telephoned police. Shortly after, he met a team of detectives in Center City and was taken to Homicide. Later, his wife appeared. She said she had been separated from Maleno for the past several months. She tried to see him at Homicide, but was instructed she couldn't. She told reporters that her husband was an unemployed sheet-metal worker. She claimed they had a four-year-old son.

At the arraignment room of police headquarters, a cop warns a United Press photographer that he is not to take photos inside the courtroom. Nevertheless, the photographer hunches near an elevator, four yards away from a gate that separates free men from confined. I stand near the photographer, hoping to get a glimpse of Maleno as he enters the courtroom.

About 1 A.M., the elevator door opens. Flashes pop, momentarily blinding the accused. He squints, lowers his eyes to the floor. Two burly officers guard him—bookends on each side. A reporter, who obviously has seen *The Front Page* too many times, gets close and blurts, "Did you kill John Knight?" Maleno and bookends keep moving.

In the courtroom, the judge asks Maleno if he has an attorney, then tells the prisoner that he will be held without bail.

Maleno looks as if he's been hit by a bulldozer. He is clad in a raincoat that's been through hurricanes. Tan slacks in need of pressing peek out from the bottom of the coat. The unshaven face of a street-wise punk sticks out from the top.

"Sign this document," says the judge.

"I can't," snaps Maleno, eyeing his handcuffs.

An officer removes the manacles and Maleno signs the paper. On his way out, the full press brigade follows and flashbulbs snap as if the Queen Mother were visiting town. But this time Maleno stares straight ahead.

"Who killed John Knight?" asks the Hildy Johnson type.

"Go fuck yourself," spits Maleno as the elevator door slams in the reporter's face.

There's an old newspaper saying that front-page stories are easier to come by during the month of August and the two or three weeks preceding Christmas. Normally, very little happens in the news then, and city editors are likely to milk a sensational piece long past its prescribed course. Typical was the death of Marilyn Monroe in August 1962. The *New York Times*, which usually shies away from suicides and sensationalism, bannered the story for two weeks. It's not surprising, then, that John Knight's murder almost erases all political news from the front pages of Philadelphia dailies, including the *News* and the *Inquirer*—papers which are part of the Knight-Ridder chain owned by the murdered man's grandfather. For two weeks following Knight's stabbing, media has a field day.

Columnists at the *News* who knew John write odes. Larry McMullen claims, "I thought he was a simple guy. Now that he's dead, I realize that nobody is that easy to figure out." Jonathan Takiff, the *News* theater critic, pans *Murder Among Friends*, a Janet Leigh play which opened the night following Knight's death. "The last thing I wanted to see was a murder mystery with frivolous comic overtones. . . . Never have I felt that killing was amusing. And just now, the tragic senseless death of a friend and fellow newspaperman has left me baffled, bitter and shocked."

Knight's death is shocking, the circumstances behind the killing macabre, and the underlying social implications horrifying.

The murder took place Sunday morning, December 7, 1975. It climaxed an evening that started innocently enough with a dinner party at La Truffe, which Knight himself had hosted. His guests were Ellen Roche (a friend who worked at a bank), Mr. and Mrs. Paul Janensch (Janensch is managing editor at the *News* and was Knight's boss), and Dr. and Mrs. John McKinnon.

If there was a purpose to the occasion, it was to celebrate the McKinnons' visit to Philadelphia. McKinnon and Knight had been roommates in Cambridge in the late sixties and had kept in touch through the years. In fact, Knight was best man at the McKinnons' wedding, but the McKinnons had not visited Knight since he moved to Philadelphia more than a year before. They had planned to stay the weekend as his houseguests, to be shown around the city by John, to generally have a whiz-bang time of it all.

Earlier that day, they had checked into Knight's apartment, rested, seen a bit of the town, had a couple of cocktails, then ambled off to La Truffe. Dinner consisted of four pheasants which John had shot in South Dakota a couple of months before and which the restaurant had prepared especially for him and his guests.

As usual, there was plenty to drink, and John played the debonair host as he suggested the best scotch before dinner, rare wines with each course, and cordials to climax the gourmet meal. Conversation was light, sometimes sparkling; no one got drunk; giddy perhaps, but in full control.

At 12:20 A.M., the Janensches said good night and took Ellen Roche to her car, leaving Knight and the McKinnons free to return to his Rittenhouse Square apartment.

Once home, Dr. McKinnon and Knight drank brandy and reminisced about the old days—and Rosemary McKinnon dozed off on her husband's lap. Shortly after 1 A.M., the phone rang. John answered, spoke to the caller softly, but with more than a hint of annoyance in his voice. The doctor overheard part of the conversation. He heard John say, "I can't see you tonight. I've got houseguests."

When John hung up the phone, he explained casually to Dr. McKinnon that the call was from a procurer who set him up with girls. It was an explanation that needn't have been made, and one which embarrassed the rather proper doctor.

About 3 A.M., the phone rang again. John was more abrupt with the caller this time. After hanging up, he suggested that the McKinnons retire to the guest room.

Dr. McKinnon speculated that John might be having a girl come by. He and his wife bade their chum good night—both men were quite smashed by then—and shuffled off to bed.

At 4 A.M., the doorbell rang. Knight answered: it was

the phone caller. Knight explained he couldn't let him
in, but the caller made a ruckus in the hallway,
pleading, "I love you, John. I must see you."

Eventually, Knight opened the door. The man pushed
past him. The man was Felix Melendez, accompanied by
Steven Maleno and Salvatore Soli.

They forced Knight to his bedroom. Even with his
paunch, John Knight was strong as an ox and didn't
give in easily. Still, he was tipsy. His targets were not
easily discernible. They overpowered him. One of them
knocked his head against a Ming vase. Once he was
down, they used belts and ropes and socks to tie his legs
together and bind his hands behind his back. They
gagged his mouth with his best silk neckties.

Then they ransacked the apartment. In the guest
room, they discovered the McKinnons. Rosemary
McKinnon was ordered naked from the bed. Dr.
McKinnon was unbudgeable. Too many drinks—he was
out like a light. The men did not force him to awaken.
Instead, Salvatore Soli made Mrs. McKinnon walk
through the apartment, open desk drawers and assist
him in the search for valuables. Rosemary McKinnon
remembers that Soli had a handgun and that Felix
Melendez roamed the apartment with a harpoon gun
and a scuba-diving knife. When she and Soli reached
Knight's bedroom, she saw her host lying face down in
the corner. He was not moving.

Ninety minutes into the chaos, the apartment doorbell rang. It was the Dorchester's night attendant, who
had come to report that a neighbor was complaining
that she couldn't sleep due to the noise. Felix Melendez
told the attendant that he was Knight's brother-in-law
and that the two were practicing karate. The attendant
suggested that they practice during the day.

The call frightened Maleno and Soli and they decided
to flee with the goods they had collected. They tied up

Mrs. McKinnon and placed her under a living room sofa. Melendez was left in the apartment. He was extremely nervous, pacing, muttering to himself. Each time he saw Mrs. McKinnon in her prone position, he danced an imperfect gavotte, wheeling and turning, unsure of the next step to take. Finally, Rosemary McKinnon persuaded him to untie her. As soon as he did, she ran to the guest room, grabbed one of her host's hunting rifles, woke her husband, gave the rifle to him, and hurriedly but lucidly explained what had happened. The explanation was more sobering than forty cups of black coffee. The doctor rushed into Knight's bedroom. Knight seemed to be dead. The doctor gave him mouth-to-mouth resuscitation. As he leaned back from his efforts, he saw Melendez standing on Knight's bed. "I didn't do it, I didn't do it," Melendez screamed. He was holding a spear gun and a scuba-diving knife. McKinnon wrestled with him, but Melendez eased his way out of the doctor's stranglehold and fled the apartment.

Meanwhile, Rosemary McKinnon, now discreetly covered by a robe, had escaped to the outside hallway, where she waited for an elevator to take her to the main lobby and safety. Just as the elevator stopped, Melendez leaped into the car with her. They tussled. He knicked her under the breast with the knife. At the third floor, the elevator came to a halt and Mrs. McKinnon ran out and down the fire escape. By the time the police arrived, Melendez had vanished.

Five days later—just an hour after Steven Maleno's arraignment—the news breaks. Felix Melendez, too, is dead.

Melendez and Knight: the hustler and the heir. Yesterday I hadn't heard of either of them, much less the McKinnons, Maleno and Soli. Suddenly, I find the Knight case the focal point of my life.

That evening, I check the four-star specials at the Warwick Hotel's newsstand. Melendez's face is splattered all over the pages. "KNIGHT SUSPECT SHOT TO DEATH: BODY FOUND IN JERSEY." For some strange reason, an old song recorded by Lee Wiley rings through my head: "Love laughs at a king, Kings don't mean a thing, On the street of dreams."

In a melancholy mood, I head toward Philadelphia's street of dreams.

Tonight, Spruce Street is bare. Since the cops put the heat on, most of the hustlers who hang out near Corson's Pharmacy are home with their mamas addressing Christmas cards. Across the street from the Drake Hotel, I find a bare stoop and settle in. A police car passes twice and finally stops. The officer requests identification. I show him my reliable press badge and ask if this is his regular beat. Had he bumped into Felix Melendez during his travels? "I'm not talking to you guys," he replies, satisfied of my legitimacy but lecturing that press privileges do not include loitering. I shrug him off, continue to loiter, and play the village idiot, pumping the not-so-innocent who stop for sidewalk conversation.

Long past midnight, a short, fidgety type dumps his wares beside me and begins a soliloquy. Somewhere between proclaiming that he's a starving hustler, long at it, familiar with the tricks of the trade, thinking of retiring to a soft job like working the stationery counter at Wanamaker's, the man swears up and down the Liberty Bell that he and Felix Melendez had made it. "I knew both Melendez and Knight," he says. "Lots of us did. Melendez started playing the street last summer. He was very hot—a face and body to stop traffic. Kind of innocent, too. His father was a priest."

Knight he calls "a closet queen."

"Whenever I saw him, he had a jacket over his head

and a chicken by his side. The last couple of months, the chicken was Felix.''

He continues that Knight used to be a regular at the 247 Club and suggests I check it out.

Close to closing, I enter the 247, which is just across the street from the Warwick. The bar is pseudo S & M, which means that it tries but doesn't quite succeed. Vinyl, as opposed to leather. Stances, instead of stunts. I amble up to the bar. Place myself near a distinguished-looking cowboy. Ask the man if he's been following the Knight murder case.

"Was there a killing?" he responds. "I've only been here a week. I'm from Baltimore. My business is in Baltimore. How terrible. A homosexual murder?" He lights a Salem and gazes blankly in the direction of the Royal Flush pinball machine. Paranoia gets the best of me. Could he be a reporter from the *Baltimore Sun*? Or the *New York Times*? I smile, and move on to a younger man dressed in flannel and jeans.

"Do you live in Philadelphia?"

"Yes," he replies.

"Come here often?"

"I'm a Republican and I don't have much time for fun."

He shrugs and slips into a sotto voce pontification on the state of hustlers, talking about gay people in the third person plural. "Keep away from hustlers," he advises. "Gay people are unreliable."

I'm not sure whether he's serious or joking. He asks if I'm gay.

"What do you think?"

"Are you political?"

"Yes and no."

"Good."

He gulps down his last dreg of Schlitz and walks out the door.

Feeling like a fish out of water, I stare at my soda glass. Standing alone for a while, I become increasingly depressed. I ask the bartender if I can have a word with him. He stops polishing the counter. His moustache is the grandson of Jerry Colonna's. Had he seen Knight during his many visits to the 247? "I don't know what you're talking about," snaps the bartender. He turns his back and continues polishing. I'm left alone at the bar, except for three gigglers and a Hell's Angels candidate. "What I Did for Love" blares from the jukebox.

Ritualistic? The coroner's report indicates that there were four stab wounds in John Knight's back. One in the chest. Three of the wounds may not have been immediately fatal. Two were definitely. Back wounds cut through the victim's arteries. Front wound penetrated the heart, leaving a gaping hole.

Four of the five wounds could have been inflicted while the victim's hands were tied. One wound would not have been possible if Knight's hands were tied behind his back, meaning that it was inflicted before the victim was bound. Stabbings could have taken place at five-minute intervals.

Bruises on face and head caused by the impact of blunt instruments. Minimum seven heavy blows. Wounds on each side of the head, on cheeks, around eyes.

Analysis of urine and liver showed traces of alcohol. Possibly ten ounces of one hundred proof consumed within the hour. No traces of narcotics, drugs, chemicals, or poisons.

Dry blood discovered on skin surfaces and center of John Knight's palm. Wet blood on clothing: extensive soaking of fabric material. Blood type O.

Dennis Rubini, with his gay liberation connections,

knows a lot of the "nice" young men of Philadelphia.
The "nice" young men are the men who have a social
consciousness and attend meetings at which they discuss
ways and means of getting civil rights legislation passed
so that the homosexual will no longer think of himself
as a second-class citizen.

Dennis Rubini has never seen John Knight at any of
these meetings. No one has, because Knight has never
been to one. Most of the time, Knight thought of himself as straight. The "gay" thing was that part of the
psyche you kept in the closet along with three fur coats.

Rubini suggests that I socialize with some of the
"nice" young men. "We don't all wear mink," he says.
"We Philadelphians are not all heirs—or hustlers, for
that matter." He gives me the names of a few hangouts
where the liberated meet and eat. At one of these spots,
a Central City pizza heaven, I speak to a nice young
man with sort of upside-down eyes and an interesting
pout. The young man tells me that he studied art at
Brown, moved to Philadelphia two years ago, and is
earning a shitty salary as a florist in a fancy shop. He
lives on Pine, near Twentieth, in the heart of the gay
ghetto, three blocks away from the Dorchester.

After thirty minutes of geranium talk, I ask him to
return to the Warwick with me. He retorts, "I don't like
hotels," and invites me to see his Venus's-flytrap. We
head toward his apartment. En route, he offers his un-
professional analysis on matters concerning the social
structure of Philadelphia: who associates with whom
and why, what the residents of King of Prussia don't
have in common with the folk of Society Hill. Florists
do get around.

In his bedroom, with three candles burning, we make
love. He's anxious to please—almost too anxious. I
climax too fast. We continue for another hour. He cannot come. Finally, he stops trying, and assures me that it

doesn't matter. "There must be something wrong with me tonight," he says.

He fetches two wineglasses and a bottle of vodka from the kitchen. Drinking makes him talkative. Very talkative. Personal stuff, problems with employer—mistreated, misused. Ironically, he has a roundabout connection to John Knight. Seems he occasionally does floral arrangements for an interior designer named Andrew Liberty. Liberty, allegedly, was Knight's closest friend in Philadelphia and had been extensively quoted in the dailies the day after the killing. Ironically, too, my new friend is oblivious to the Knight mess. He is not a newspaper reader and television is mainly old movies and the talk shows. The sudden intrusion of a New York journalist hotly trailing the story of a murdered in-the-closet gay brings excitement to his life. He calls Andrew Liberty, but not before lecturing about the kind of affected interior-decorator type of mentality that lies in store.

Perhaps elitism reigns within the design field. Perhaps florists and decorators don't sip brandy from the same goldfish snifter. But the next night when we visit Liberty, I do not find him a first-class snob. I do find that Liberty prefers the prettier ornaments of life, such as the young man he is presently living with, the car they drive, and the house they live in.

Liberty and his live-in companion pick up the florist and me and drive us to their house in Society Hill, in a BMW Bavaria. A Nevelson sculpture dominates the living room. The light from the fireplace makes Liberty look like a mop-topped juvenile. He's probably thirty, though: he's been around too long to be less. Somewhere along the line he has married a socialite and sired a son. He works for Dorothy Lerner, a decorator who is irate because Andy's name has been bandied about in the papers. The notoriety, she fears, will set the jowls of her clientele aquiver.

With a drink in one hand, Liberty motions me to a corner of the room away from our two companions. He speaks cautiously at first, not certain how far he should go.

He claims that he met John Knight when Knight first moved to Philadelphia in September 1974. Knight rented two adjacent Dorchester apartments—a three- and a two-bedroom—and had elaborate ideas about coordination. Knight wanted to knock the walls down and go for neutral colors as backdrop for his extensive art collection. He wanted to convert one room into a gym.

Liberty suggested that he throw out his old heavy furniture. Why not take advantage of the huge windows which overlook Rittenhouse Square park and all Philadelphia? Use the city as backdrop for understated furnishings.

At the time, John Knight struck Andrew Liberty as sophisticated, but not ostentatious. Knight's clothes were quality and English-tailored but well worn, lived in. With his moist eyes, his well-nourished 174-pound frame indiscreetly distributed over his five-foot ten-inch body, he resembled a Teddy bear and acted slightly reticent. Knight told Liberty that he knew no one in Philadelphia. They struck up an immediate friendship.

They began lunching at the Latham. Three-hour talks that began with furniture, shifted to psychology, and ended with self-revelation. Layers of Knight's personality unfolded. He told Liberty about his background at Harvard and Oxford, about his travels, about the call he received from an anonymous tipster when he was working the newsroom at the *Detroit Free Press*. The call described the mental problems of then Democratic vice-presidential candidate Senator Thomas Eagleton. Knight instituted a series of articles which forced Eagleton off the McGovern ticket and won the Knight-Ridder papers a Pulitzer Prize.

As their friendship developed, Knight opened up about his relationship with his grandfather. The old man worshiped him and clearly wanted young John to take over the newspaper chain. But first he insisted that his grandson learn the business from the ground up. So, at the *Detroit Free Press*, Knight delivered papers by truck to familiarize himself with routing. He covered the police beat, wrote editorial copy, and toiled in advertising, which he hated, always keeping in touch with granddad, like a kid showing A's on a report card to his parents. The two Knights didn't see each other too often. Once, John invited Andy Liberty to accompany him on a visit to his grandfather's winter estate in Bal Harbor, Florida, but the visit fell through.

In Philadelphia, young John earned a weekly salary of $350 and worked eight-hour shifts. He moonlighted a review of the Rolling Stones when they played town, an achievement he was exceedingly proud of. Music was his love, just as hunting was his hobby (he could not shoot deer because he couldn't stand to see the whites of their eyes), weight lifting his *tsuris* (the weight problem was constant, but Knight could bench-press 250) and cooking his way of communicating.

Two weeks before his death, John Knight had Andrew Liberty and his friend up for "the best breakfast of my life: freshly squeezed orange juice with Dom Pérignon, Canadian bacon, filet mignon and eggs, coffee." Generous to a fault, Knight nevertheless was shrewd with money. He traded his speedboat for an original Picasso print on the theory that the boat would depreciate while the Picasso increased in value. Money meant security. Lately he felt very secure: his

Philadelphia bank account showed a total of a million and a half. Rarely did he keep more than two hundred in cash at the apartment. He drove a workingman's 1972 Grand Prix. Politically, he was liberal, leaning toward conservative rather than radical. His upbringing was Republican. Grandpa was a Nixon supporter until the 1972 election. In a conspicuous spot in a walk-in closet, John Knight kept a photo of himself with Nixon. That it was kept in the closet, Liberty thinks, was a statement.

And then there was the gay thing. "I suspected it," claims Liberty. "He was beating around the bush and I brought it up. One night John said, 'Look, I'm new in town, I'm a newspaperman, I should know the night-clubs. You know them. Why not take me around?'

"I said, 'John, what gay clubs do you want to see first?'" So we went on a tour: the Steps, Allegro, the PBL. We drank and talked and danced a little but there was a holding back. John compartmentalized himself. His life was like a long hallway with a lot of closets. None of the closets were connected and each time he would have to go back to the hallway to get from one to the other."

Obviously homosexuality was a problem that gnawed at Knight. It bothered him because of his stature and the possibility that if Grandpa found out, he'd get cut off. Consequently, he dated "respectable" women. Bright women who were his social equals. Eventually, he thought he'd marry.

The men he dated were overaged children he wouldn't be caught dead with in a social situation. He'd find a poor waif, and father him. Knight's own father died in the Battle of the Bulge a couple of weeks before he was born. He never had a father, so some kind of reverse transference was a factor in his relationships with males. He looked for the baby face and the big blue eyes. If

they didn't speak proper English and were poverty-
stricken, they'd get points. Knight would take them to
the Dorchester, give them food, let them fool around
with his stereo and camera equipment, talk to them like
a father, wrestle with them—and then came the nitty-
gritty part where paternalism took the form of incest.
Never would Knight seek out a male peer as a sexual
partner. Affluent, intelligent homosexual men were
avoided, even as friends. Andrew Liberty was the ex-
ception.

John Knight knew that the sexual part of his life was
fly-by-night, destructive, impossible to reconcile even
with the help of an analyst. The truth is, he
acknowledged the hypocrisy of his life.

The night before his death, Knight phoned Liberty
and asked him to come over to watch *Tora! Tora! Tora!*
on television. When the film ended, Knight bubbled like
a schoolboy because his old buddy McKinnon would be
visiting with his wife, Rosemary, and they'd be staying
with him for the weekend. He assured Liberty that
McKinnon was straighter than an arrow. Would Liberty
join the party for dinner the following night?

Andrew Liberty said he'd love to but had another
engagement. At 2 A.M., he bade his last goodbye to his
friend.

Early Sunday morning, the phone rang with the news
that John Knight had been murdered. Liberty thought
the call was a joke. But he drove to the Dorchester, just
in case. When he arrived, he knew there was nothing to
laugh about. The first words from the police were, "Did
you know John Knight was a homosexual?"

They let him enter Knight's apartment. The place was
in a shambles. Furniture that Liberty had carefully
selected was destroyed. Blood on the navy blue rug.
Metal lamps crushed. Plants torn. Clothes scattered.
Glass shattered.

"The stench of death surrounded me," says Liberty, "and my reaction was hate. I lost my orientation. I got sick. Two days ago, we were sitting here, drinking champagne."

Andrew and his friend offer to drive us back to the florist's apartment. Quiet. Christmas trees in store fronts. We stop for coffee at an existentialist-style restaurant in the bohemian part of town. Liberty is no longer moping about his departed friend. He drops names of New York interior designers and speaks about shows he has seen, restaurants he has visited, clothes, styles, acquisitions, men, models, and media. At home, my florist friend complains that Liberty is the walking stereotype of an interior designer. "I told you," he says. "I don't like him. It's like he's making Knight's death into a star vehicle for himself."

And I think to myself of assignments where another's tragedy had indeed been a vehicle for self-promotion. While covering the Dean Corll murders in Houston, I interviewed the mother of one of the victims. Her son had been missing for eighteen months and the woman had long assumed him to be dead: the police revelations of the multiple murders confirmed her suspicions. At her little house in the Heights section, she pulled out valentines from a trunk to show me: cards the young boy had long ago sent, telling Mama how wonderful she was. That was the theme. How wonderful the boy was because he thought she was so wonderful. She told about all the wonderful things she had done for him. Then between valentine greetings, she posed dramatically for the photographer, making sure he got her best profile, keeping her head tilted upward to remove any sign of a double chin. Bravery, in face of the camera. Her parting shot was "Will it be a cover story?"

• • •

The *Philadelphia News* and *Inquirer* building is within walking distance of City Hall, my geographical point of reference in the city of brotherly turmoil. On the editorial floor of the *News*, a police radio blares and ten phones ring at once. "There's no one in the sports department," grumbles a reporter to one of the phone receivers, then yells, "Who are you waiting for?"

"Paul Janensch," I answer.

"In there." She points to an inner office.

Janensch is in his mid-thirties. He looks like he loves the great indoors: that gray-pink pallor which comes from too much time spent under fluorescent lighting is a color common to editors. Horn-rimmed glasses are perched on the bridge of his nose. He leans back in his swivel chair, hands behind his head, and snaps that he's already said probably all there is to say about his last supper with Knight at La Truffe. "Have you read our coverage?"

I answer, "Every last word of it."

"Well, then anything I tell you is redundant. The meal was one of the most pleasant I've had in a long time. It lasted four hours. John selected the wines. The wine tab alone came to $114. The McKinnons were good company. So was Ellen Roche. She was simply a friend of John's. No romance. So far as I could tell, their relationship was one of friendship."

Did Janensch have any idea of Knight's sexual orientation?

"You mean did I suspect that John was gay? No, I didn't. There was never a thought in my mind about John being homosexual—that night, or ever. I've worked closely with him. On two occasions, I had bumped into him socially—each time with a different woman. I always saw him with people from the straight world. Everybody who knew John thought he was totally straight. We were utterly amazed at these revelations.''

Would Janensch care to comment on a newspaper report that Felix Melendez knew that the McKinnons were set to spend the weekend with John, that Melendez suspected Knight and McKinnon of being lovers, and killed Knight in a jealous rage?

''Judging from the few hours we spent together, there was no indication of a homosexual relationship between McKinnon and Knight,'' says Janensch. ''None at all. Theirs was nothing more than a conventional friendship.''

Janensch had been employed by the *Louisville Courier-Journal* before becoming managing editor of the *Philadelphia News*. He had worked with John Knight since November 1974: Knight had been the *News*'s day editor but was to have started a new job in a couple of weeks as project director of the paper's late edition. It was to be Knight's baby. Completely. This would be the chance to show his grandfather he could soar.

''John came to Philadelphia because he wanted a change of scene from the *Detroit Free Press*, where he was stagnating,'' offers Janensch. ''Philadelphia is where the action is. It is the most competitive newspaper city in the country. And the *News* is the only tabloid of its kind in town. That the paper is vulgar, brash, and urban-oriented attracted John.''

All along, Knight kept a ''low profile'' at the *News*. Had Janensch been unaware of the family connection, he suspects he'd still have spotted money. Not that John was throwing it around—he wasn't ostentatious—but often the working rich are twice as conscientious as the working middle class. They have to prove that they deserve their jobs in spite of their inherited status because privilege is nothing you earn.

"John often worked fourteen-hour shifts. If a big story came his way, he kept his cool. He could handle it." Those few times when Janensch saw John "manic" were, oddly enough, when he was working on articles of minor significance, stories way below his capabilities. Imagination was there—in spades. For instance, when New York City was about to fall because of its fiscal crisis, Knight and an artist worked out a composite photo of the Statue of Liberty sinking in the harbor. When news broke about the C.I.A.'s aborted attempts to assassinate Castro, John suggested that the paper run an illustration of the Cuban revolutionary, eyes wide with shock, hair falling out, accompanied by a balloon explaining "Caramba!" They did. On the front page.

His nose for news, in Janensch's opinion, could eventually have made him the bona fide successor to Granddad Knight *despite* the aid of nepotism. Like the old man, John's view didn't particularly follow a straight line. He was for abortion, but also for capital punishment. He was against the Vietnam War but conservative on fiscal matters. As far as the gay issue is concerned, journalistically, he kept away from it. "The paper has not come out against gay rights," says Janensch, "but we have an active invisible gay life here in Philadelphia, one that is not especially kinky. And we are sympathetic to the demands of these gay groups. We offer them maximum opportunity to tell their side of the story.

"This gay movement stuff wasn't John's territory to cover. It wasn't an issue. However, I think if John's grandfather discovered his tendencies, he'd certainly be upset, but I doubt if he'd do anything drastic. He'd probably want to help John and send him to a psychoanalyst."

I leave Janensch's office wondering why I didn't tell him I'm gay? Why shouldn't he know it? Or is what I do

in bed irrelevant in matters outside the bedroom?
Perhaps a homosexual's skin should be a different
color. Lavender for immediate identification. Would it
have changed matters any had Janensch and his co-
workers known about Knight? Does the sound of
money in conjunction with clout and power negate
one's sexual orientation? Does intelligence, a low
profile, and playing it cool make one acceptable? What
if John Knight were lavender?

John Knight's life—and death—is getting to me.

No way the Knight story will be ready for the next
issue of the *Voice*. I'm too involved to want to go back
to New York right away, so decide to interview Janet
Leigh in Philadelphia for my weekly column.

The former movie star is staying at the Bellevue-
Stratford Hotel. A couple of days ago, she came down
with some kind of stomach virus which hospitalized her
and kept her out of *Murder Among Friends* for two per-
formances. But she's back rehearsing—the show is supposed to be in bad trouble and needs fixing before its
New York opening. Janet's teenage daughter, Tracy,
keeps me entertained at the hotel while we both wait for
mother.

Sparkling Tracy. From Beverly Hills. Making light
conversation. "Wanamaker's was awful this afternoon," she sighs. "I was pushed and stared at by
smelly old men. Ugh. Philadelphia stinks. Terrible
town. Mommy can't wait to get back to tennis in
California."

Mommy finally arrives, twenty minutes late—apolo-
getic, snippy and bored. I can't get much out of her.
She's probably done similar interviews a million times
before—discovered by Norma Shearer, past marriage to
Tony Curtis, friendship with Howard Hughes, career
boost with Hitchcock's *Psycho*.

She claims that she prefers making movies with a little less gutter realism than we're getting nowadays. "There's a place for all kinds of films," she argues, "from Walt Disney to Andy Warhol, but I like coming out of a theater feeling good, not bad. Entertainment turns me on. I get enough realism reading the papers."

Has the actress read the papers about the Knight murder? "Yes. My play opened when the news of the murder broke and the critics were in no frame of mind to look at a vehicle that deals with murder. In some awful way, my play parallels that situation at Rittenhouse Square."

In what awful way?

"I can't tell you," she answers. "The play is a mystery. See for yourself. But don't see it yet. Wait until it comes to New York. This much I can tell you. One of the characters is a homosexual."

(When it came to New York, *Murder Among Friends* played a week—the critics used butcher knives to cut it to shreds. I missed the play and got a bland column out of Janet Leigh. Both our heads were elsewhere.)

Felix Melendez's body was discovered near the entranceway to the Pine Valley Golf Club near Camden, New Jersey, at 8:45 A.M., Friday, December 11, 1975. The body was found in a clump of woods by a caddy on his way to work. The caddy summoned a guard at the club gatehouse who called the police. Shortly afterward, the site was swarming with F.B.I. agents and homicide detectives.

Two gunshot wounds had penetrated Melendez. One was in the back of his head, the other in one of his cheeks. Melendez was lying on his back about a hundred feet up a road that leads to a Boy Scout reservation. His head pointed toward the road, his feet toward the trunk of a tree. One arm was stretched rigidly in the air. On its wrist dangled a silver bracelet.

He was outfitted in a long-sleeved white sport shirt and brown pants. A black vinyl wallet was found in his left hip pocket. Among its contents: a lunch ticket from the School District of Philadelphia, a welfare identification card, a social security card, a driver's license, a public library card, and an alcohol influence chart.

Samples of the victim's hair, fingernails, and metal fragments from his skull were taken to the state police lab. So were his black socks and his black-leather Elliot brand boots. Although jacketless and coatless, Felix Melendez died with his boots on.

Those who knew Felix well claim he preferred high-heeled platform shoes, the kind that were trendy in the early seventies but out of vogue by the time they reached his attention. He dressed "jazzy" when he had the money. "Fruity," some said. Pegged pants and vivid colors. Partial to glitter at night.

Sweet kid, though. Everyone thought so. His neighborhood buddies thought so. The woman whose baby he fathered thought so. Sweet, but fucked up.

"He was wild and he liked to play around," says Elias Melendez, Felix's eighteen-year-old brother, as he sits in a dark City Hall vestibule, his seventeen-year-old wife, Nancy, silent by his side.

Felix was born on November 20, 1955, in a transient North Philadelphia neighborhood, the son of an itinerent Pentecostal minister from Puerto Rico. He was the second son. Elias was the third. There would be two more sons, then two daughters, then two more sons born during the years the elder Melendez worked at odd jobs and preached at the local church.

"When we were growing up," Elias remembers, "Felix was very active. He liked to horse around, so, naturally, he got blamed for everything by our parents. He developed a complex and believed everyone was persecuting him, that if anything went wrong, he was the one who did it.

"In school, he used to get in and out of trouble and was suspended a lot. At Edison High, he stayed only six days, then dropped out."

In 1972, the boys' father became assistant pastor of Rose of Sharon Pentecostal Church and insisted that Felix attend services regularly. Felix balked. He left home. To support himself, he took a number of menial jobs like cleaning tables at a Center City restaurant and pumping gas at a suburban garage. For a short while, Felix and Elias worked together as stock boys at Christopher's Auto Parts.

"The phone was always ringing for him," recalls Elias. "Always the girls. So much, he nearly got fired. Felix was very good-looking and the girls were always chasing him."

One nearly caught up. In 1972, Felix met Donna Leone, the daughter of a truck driver, at the home of a friend. They started dating. For the first time in a long while, Felix felt good about himself. He got a job at a Youth Corps center in South Philadelphia and returned to school at night to obtain a graduate equivalent certificate.

During those moments when he was not "bettering" himself, he and Donna played Romeo and Juliet, Philadelphia style. They talked marriage, but Donna's father told them to wait until Felix made something of himself.

"Donna's father didn't like my brother," admits Elias, his head shaking as if a sin had been committed. "Felix wasn't the type of guy he wanted for his daughter. Sure, my brother wanted to marry Donna, but he also wanted to hang around with other girls. He really didn't want to settle down but he didn't want to be wild either. He didn't know what he wanted.

"He was high-strung. He took a lot of pills. A couple of times the police picked him up from the ground because they found him like he was having an epileptic fit. I think it was a nerve attack."

In February 1973, Felix and Elias found themselves the only members of the Melendez family left in Philadelphia. An uncle who was a minister died in Puerto Rico. Their father returned to the island, taking the rest of the Melendez family with him. Eventually, their father took over the dead uncle's parish.

Felix, meanwhile, fervently threw himself into the business of making something of himself. He moved into the home of an older man who owned a laundry. Even though the man was like a father to him, Felix hated the drudgery of working indoors. He wanted to be free, unrestricted by walls.

That internal pang for freedom soon manifested itself externally. Felix started seeing a lot of girls in addition to Donna.

"Girls would run after him," says Elias. "I'm sure boys did, too. The brown hair, the green eyes, he had kind of an innocent angel's face. His looks opened doors, but they were also his downfall. I can't tell you exactly when, maybe two or three years ago, he even caught a case of syphilis. He had to get an injection every day for a week before it went away.

"And he got into trouble for reckless driving. Felix got picked up once for having a knife on him. It was his protection, like his rosary beads. He liked to pick a fight, but he'd usually run away.

"One time he didn't, though. I had a girl friend who he didn't like. Felix called her a whore. So I ran after him. We got into a fistfight. It's the only time I've seen Felix violent."

What about drugs? How often did Felix get high? Did he drop acid? Snort coke?

"I don't know. He used to lie so much to me that I wouldn't believe him when he told me the truth. He loved to lie."

Tears fill Elias Melendez's eyes as he talks. His wife takes his hand. Her other hand pats the nape of his neck. There are times when I wish I were in another profession, like tie dying or tap dancing. This is one of them.

I ask Elias if he'd rather not continue to reminisce.

"No. It's okay. You are bringing back memories. Things I haven't thought about in a long time.

"Donna gave birth to Felix's baby in November 1974, a little girl named Faith. The decent thing for Felix to do was to marry Donna. He wanted to, but Donna didn't feel the time was right yet. They stopped seeing each other for a while. Felix moved from the home of the man who ran the laundry. He lived with me for about four months.

"I noticed he started hanging out then. I don't know exactly where he went: Center City, somewhere. I don't know whether he was gay. I never even thought about it. I was surprised when I heard he was.

"And I still can't believe it. You see, we were brought up in a Christian family where it isn't right to be homosexual. It must have hurt Felix's conscience. When he lived with me, I know many things were bothering him and I gave him a lot of advice to stay out of trouble. That last year, he couldn't seem to do anything he wanted to do. He'd get nervous and impatient and excited. He met this guy, Joe Paolucci, a baker, and moved in with him in South Philadelphia. I'd been to their house, but never met Paolucci. Felix was living there when all this trouble happened."

When Felix lived with Joe Paolucci, was there any indication that his life was different? Had there been any radical change in his behavior?

Hesitation. For a long moment, silence. Then Elias looks at his wife, whose understanding of English is spotty, and translates the question to her in Spanish. She nods her head affirmatively. Elias continues.

"He had money, that's what was different. The last few weeks, Felix would come around and say, 'Do you need cash?' He'd give me two or three dollars to help me out. I don't know where he got the money, but he was dressing better, too. Lots of new flashy clothes. I knew he was still taking those pills because he looked glassy-eyed. He had to be on something.

"He never confided that his life was any different than it had been. And he never mentioned John Knight. Never. That much I'll tell you.

"In November, our mother came to visit us from Puerto Rico. She stayed at my house and Felix dropped by a few times. He told our mother that he was studying to be a lawyer. I knew he was lying but it made her happy.

"We went out a few times and everything seemed fine. Felix came with me to the airport to see our mother off. That was the last time I saw him—less than a week before he was killed. The last words I remember from Felix were that one day he would be somebody. 'Just wait and see,' he said. 'Just wait and see.' "

A faded blue poster of the Virgin Mary holding the baby Jesus decorates the saloon window at the corner where I get off the South Philadelphia bus. The poster announces a rummage sale at the Church of Our Lady of Something or Other. South Philadelphia is crawling with churches. And three-story houses identical in design that form a monotonous architecture interrupted only by a candy store or a social club or a school. The houses are immaculate. Old Italian women spend hours scrubbing and sweeping their parcels of concrete and asphalt.

Mayor Frank Rizzo hails from South Philly. He's a former cop, the big hero, and idol of the community, the local boy who made good. They love it when he returns in a limousine and waves at them.

"Rizzo claims he supports a gay rights bill," says the gay activist resident of South Philly who has volunteered to guide me around the neighborhood. He elaborates that Rizzo has been unable to get the bill passed, which is a curiosity since the mayor's power is strong enough to allow a recently deceased city councilman to run for office. The man was one of Rizzo's allies. Rizzo doesn't forget a favor—even if they're dead. And believe it or not, the dead man won the race.

Family honor is big in South Philadelphia. People protect their relatives. Call someone's sister a whore and you'll find your head bashed in.

No big deal is made of the Mafia. They support the community. Better the Mafia than the liberal politicians, is the feeling. Tradition has it that a young man "investigates" the Mafia about the time he has his first lay. Some of the great hoods in the city hail from South Philadelphia.

Everyone accepts the drug problem. There's not much you can do about it. Few accept blacks. On the block where my activist guide lives, a black family moved in. "Nigger" was painted on their front door. The family moved out after six months.

Homosexuality in South Philadelphia means drag queens. They're spottable, they wear their gayness on the outside, and they're accepted as freaks of nature. The toughs protect them. They banter with them. "Hey, sweetie, who's your date for tonight? Wanna give me a blow job?"

"It's not big enough, honey. I want a real man."

A man who is homosexual but dresses like everyone else and passes is a threat. If a member of a South Philadelphia gang is suddenly discovered hanging out with a homosexual for reasons other than hustling, procuring, or beating the daylights out of him, his contemporaries most likely would rough him up and banish him forever from the paternal breast. Naturally, the church doesn't like fairies. They're an abomination. It's right there in the Bible. Check Leviticus. In South Philadelphia, machismo is all.

Early noon. My guide is quick to point out that nothing happens before nightfall. We pass the saloon where Maleno hung out. Empty. We stop to examine the house where Felix Melendez lived with Joe Paolucci. Deserted. The blinds are drawn at the home of Salvatore Soli's parents. Are they watching television? Is Mrs. Soli waiting for the phone to ring with news that her son has given himself up or has been captured—or killed?

Behind each doorway, a drama.

William Randolph Hearst had Marion Davies, Daddy Browning had his luscious Peaches, and John Knight had Billy Sage long before he met Felix Melendez.

Two days after the murder, big blond Billy from Detroit showed his overripe body and baby-boy face at Rittenhouse Square, claiming he was the true love, the only love of John Knight's life. He had heard about the murder on a radio at his home in the Detroit suburbs, bought a plane ticket with his own money, hastened to Philadelphia, and appeared at the Knight digs making like the widow of a daddy who died too suddenly to remember his sugar in his will.

Sage, now twenty, expressed his grief and was only too happy to speak of a relationship that began when he was sixteen—a relationship others were to expound on in the months to come.

Billy Sage boasted about how he taught Knight to "be aware," how he always beat Knight at wrestling because he himself was stronger, how Knight "financed" him and put him through school and generally played Professor Higgins to his Eliza Doolittle.

"For four years, I tried to get John to quit his interest in other guys," Sage told a reporter from *Philadelphia Magazine*. "We were best friends. We got it on together, but that was different. After a while, that changed too. It got to be that I didn't want to think of my closest friend as some kind of gay or queer. So I wouldn't have sex with him no more. John kinda liked that, too."

As proof of their closeness, Sage led the Philadelphia police to John Knight's sealed foot locker and, with a few flicks of the wrist, opened it. Here was a veritable Pandora's box of dildoes, male-male magazines, and photographs of men with women, men with men, vertical, horizontal, in positions undreamed of by Leviticus. Among the shots were several of Billy himself: portraits saluting his manhood.

The cops did not detain Sage. Morosely, Billy decided the proper thing would be to attend his best friend's funeral. He hopped a plane to Columbus, Georgia, again paying his own transportation.

His co-passengers on the flight included a few of Knight's fellow employees at the *News* and an ex-Harvard chum who, the day before, had been asked by the Philadelphia police to look at photographs taken from Knight's locker.

Having been inundated with Kodak samplers of the big blond in all his amplitude, the school chum was infuriated by Sage's presence on the Columbus flight.

And Sage's appearance in Columbus embarrassed the Knight family.

Sage asked to be a pallbearer at the funeral. His request was denied. In fact, he was kept under constant surveillance at the chapel and graveside services by local and private police.

Knight's last rites took place at the Stiffler-Hamby Macon Road Chapel. Columbus's native son was eulogized as a "young man blessed by birth, circumstances, and family. A young man with God-given gifts." The minister explained that "there is a sense of unreality, that this man's passing is a bad dream. But it is reality. And our first thought is, Why? I can't answer. I can only comfort."

In the vestibule, police made copies of the five hundred or so signatures in the chapel guest book. After the service, mourners went by car to Parkhill Cemetery nearby. John Knight's grandfather remained in his automobile. His widowed mother, Dorothy, stood silently as the coffin was lowered. A local television news team filmed the rites from a hilly point overlooking the graveside. A wire service photographer moved among the mourners below.

In Philadelphia, plans are made to bury Felix Melendez. Two days after Knight is laid to rest, a service is held for Felix at the Urban Funeral Home on Germantown Avenue. More than 350 people, many of them curiosity seekers, come out in the freezing weather to say goodbye. Donna Leone shows up with her parents. When she approaches the open casket, she breaks down and sobs in her mother's arms. Elias Melendez remarks to all within earshot that "my brother was none of the things they say," and Donna Leone's father, in an about-face, claims, "Felix was a real good kid, trying to make good so I'd give my permission for him to marry Donna."

Determined that Felix should have a long and fitting farewell, Donna collects three hundred dollars from neighbors to go toward another viewing. It is to take place the following night at the Pullo Funeral Home in South Philadelphia.

The crowd there is smaller. No TV cameras, no media monitors visible outside the parlor. I nod solemnly at the pomaded mortician's aide at the door. He gestures for me to sign the guest book. I don't—instead, I find a seat near the back of the parlor.

The mourners are mostly young girls in miniskirts, craggy-faced mamas, babies, and teenage boys with long eyelashes and Philadelphia Flyers jackets. They occupy twenty rows of bridge chairs, which come to a halt a yard away from the casket.

Sobbing. Sobbing, everywhere. A young girl whimpers and a baby cries and another girl cries and another. Who are they? Friends of Donna Leone? Past acquaintances from the Neighborhood Center?

They make me feel out of place and I am out of place, conspicuous to myself because I shouldn't be here; somewhat guilt-ridden, because I am here. Interesting that I should feel this way among Melendez's acquaintances. Interesting that I can move comfortably, snug in the fact that I'm doing my professional duty, among Knight's peers.

I notice a plainclothesman from police headquarters. He notices me, too, but he averts his eyes from mine. Another intruder. Thank the Lord.

The place soon fills to capacity. From where I sit, it's difficult to see Felix Melendez's death face in the open coffin. There is a line of fifteen people waiting to get a view. One of the viewers is a repeater. I get in line.

Moving to the coffin is a slow process. Once there, the procedure is to look at the body for as long as you want, then get back to your seat or leave the parlor.

Most of the viewers sneak a quick glance. One viewer gazes and prays for what seems an hour. The line in back of me is long.

My turn. The coffin is plushed up with white silk satin. Melendez clad in a tan summer suit. Long and lanky. Tie tied in a tight Windsor knot. Hands folded across his chest. Hair slicked back. The cosmetician has done a remarkable job hiding whatever damage the bullet wounds had done to his countenance. Felix looks like a waxwork of Rudolph Valentino. He sports a half-smile. Or is it a silent snicker?

Enough. My eyes shift to his shoes. Cheap, with those tiny ventilation air holes. Heels in A-1 condition. Big feet. No sign of socks.

Below his feet rests a pretty heart-shaped bouquet of white gladioli. Tied to the bouquet is a card. The card reads "Daddy." That's all. "Daddy."

The gladioli and the Daddy card are buried with Felix.

THE

ESCAPE

I REMAIN IN Philadelphia for another two weeks. Days are spent tracking down leads, finding out all I can about Melendez and Knight from people who are reluctant to talk; trying to piece together parts of a jigsaw puzzle that criminologists and psychiatrists are having a tough time finishing. The missing pieces, in part, are held by the dead men.

For instance, was Felix Melendez actually jealous of Dr. McKinnon's visit with Knight? If the motive was simply robbery, why hadn't Felix broken into John's apartment before, when he knew no one else was present? Why that night of all nights?

Tales about Melendez were later to come to me from "clients" who had purchased Felix's body during those months when he was selling it. A writer who had broken up with his lover of eight years and subsequently had taken to the bottle and street encounters with strangers tells of meeting Felix in a seedy bar in the Kensington area. It's a place where Irish kids drink beer, talk tough,

47

shoot pool, brag about their "old ladies," and zero in on the odd faggot who just happens to be in the neighborhood—looking.

"I was crocked," says the author, who's in his late thirties and substandard in the looks department. "I was horny and buying drinks for anyone in sight. And getting propositioned like Carroll Baker in *The Carpetbaggers*. Believe me, it wasn't my body they wanted. But I've been around long enough to know when a proposition is a cash offer, and most of the hustlers there would just as soon cut your heart out as allow you to fuck them. They take anyone who's a fag for a sucker or a victim.

"Anyway, I was too high to care about being careful—I just wanted to cum. So when I spotted this kid with cat's eyes and black hair—I think he was the only Latin in the place—I started speaking to him. I got no response. It's like he was deep into his own thoughts but too polite to tell me to take a leap.

"I offered him a joint—he refused. A drink—he refused. Finally, I asked if he wanted to make fifty dollars. That he didn't refuse.

"We went to a rooming house—it cost me twenty dollars, and more than that in embarrassment. I told the clerk that the kid was my nephew: it's like Thelma Ritter passing Dolores Del Rio off as her niece. Once we took off our clothes, his passiveness disappeared. He was aggressive and tender and we went at it for a couple of hours. He came three times, but I couldn't climax. Not his fault—I just couldn't. When we got ready to leave, I went for my wallet and he said, 'No. I don't want any money.' I asked for his phone number. He wouldn't give it to me, but we made a date to see each other the following Saturday. He said he liked movies, so we arranged to see *Tommy*.

"All week, I looked forward to meeting Felix again.

In fact, I masturbated a couple of times at the thought of a repeat engagement, and I drank nothing. Only wine. When Saturday arrived, I got to the movie house fifteen minutes early. Felix got there thirty minutes late. He looked different. Cheap. Dressed to kill. Faggy. I wondered whether my drinking made the first meeting better than it actually was. Had I been hallucinating?

"All through *Tommy*, our legs kept touching, and, even with the queeny drag, I was dying to make it with Felix then and there. When the movie was over, we went for coffee. I asked him if he'd fuck with me again. He said, 'No, I have to work tonight.' I asked him, 'What kind of work?'—as if I had to. He answered, 'Hustling.' I offered to pay him. He said, 'No.' I never saw him after that."

Felix's experience with the writer was strikingly different from his relationship with a fabric designer. The comfortable gray-haired designer claims to have spent a month with Melendez just before he met Knight.

"Felix was a bottomless pit, constantly demanding," remembers the designer. "It was important to him that I prove time and again how much I loved him, how deeply I cared, because he didn't believe anyone could care."

As time went on, Felix became more dependent and possessive. "I tried to give him security and a sense of self, but his possessiveness was overpowering. It cut our relationship short."

One afternoon, I meet Jim Kennedy at the Hasty-Tasty Deli. Kennedy calls himself "a gay street priest who ministers to hustlers." His ministry is in the Northern Liberty area, where he lives with five young men on a two-thousand-dollar grant from the City Drug Program.

Kennedy knew Melendez slightly. Sometimes he'd

bump into Felix and John eating breakfast at the Hasty-Tasty, "but to say I knew Felix real well would be a lie. Everybody's saying that: it's like right after Martin Luther King's assassination, everyone swore they knew King."

Nevertheless, Kennedy has theories. He maintains that you must understand about class differences in order to understand the phenomenon of hustlers. The majority are working class. They come from broken homes and their feelings have been brutalized.

"Hustlers work out who they are sexually," claims Kennedy in a voice that sounds as if it's seen a lot and been a lot. "Therefore, it becomes the leitmotif of their lives. In Philadelphia, they'll range in age from thirteen to about forty-one. The older hustlers go to parties and often hang out in bars, looking for someone to keep them. If they can't succeed selling their bodies, they'll try to get a decent job. As they grow older, many of them end up picking up hustlers themselves.

"Until the Knight murder, the cops left the street hustlers alone. Their attitude was, if that's what these guys are doing, let them do it, as long as they don't hassle women on the street. Rarely was there harassment, and rarely were arrests made along Spruce.

"Felix was typical of the gang who work the street. He came from a Pentecostal background and the church is antigay. Felix had a multiple amount of oppressions working against him: religion, sexual orientation, class, and his Puerto Rican minority status."

Oppression makes curious bedfellows, and it seemed only logical that fate would bring Felix Melendez together with John Knight.

Knight sought out the street kid, the outcast, the sexual heathen, the earth child whose universe was entirely different from his. With Knight, sex was always a matter of cultural collision. "Diametrically opposed"

was a figure of speech that could elicit a hard on. He
could never sever the umbilical cord that bound him to a
patriarchal society. Cut it and there was the possibility
of Grandpa cutting him off. To go visibly against it
would be to go against everything he was ever taught in
all those fancy schools. For Knight to accept what he
was meant that he might not be accepted by the hier-
archy who expected greatness of him. Greatness meant
strength. Strength meant masculinity. Masculinity
meant heterosexuality. Heterosexuality meant façade.
Maintain façade for the world to see. Cheat in the dark
abyss of the soul. Cheat in a dimly lighted back yard.

Of course, there's no telling what might have been
had Knight played another yard. Impossible to surmise
whether he'd meet his heart's desire on the Main Line or
if he'd find a Billy Sage or Felix Melendez on Society
Hill.

The truth is, when you're rich and bothered and
restless, a hustler is easier to cope with than a sit-down
dinner for six. And with the help of a few select gay
publications, anyone can dial a whore.

They come in all shapes and colors. There are as
many varieties as there are Baskin-Robbins flavors.
Some call themselves models. They're not the runway
kind.

Hustlers who advertise in the *Advocate* (the largest
gay publication in the country) are like visiting nurses.
Many are college kids who need the bucks to get them
through school. Others are actors and dancers who
can't hold steady jobs because they need time for
auditions. Still others are lazy and find whoring a way
to pay the rent. And yet there are others with great
bodies who love sex, perform well, and figure they
might as well cash in on their hobby. They sit at home,
wait for the phone to ring, and charge the going rate.
Most male models are gay and claim to be "versatile."

Modeling is a way of meeting interesting men they wouldn't ordinarily meet. A good model is not bothered by the age, weight, height, or kinky demands of his client. He is honest: a veritable Boy Scout.

The street hustler has a tougher time of it. There's no telephone, no way of screening the crazies, no way of spotting Lilly Law in plainclothes. The pay is bad. A kid can freeze his ass off on a winter night and come home with ten dollars for a blow job. Generally, street hustlers are sexually passive. And they're younger than the house models. Pill popping and heroin are part of the scene. Homophobia is, too. Like, "I hate it, but I'm doing it and if I continue doing it, I may turn out to be, God forbid, one of them." It is not uncommon for a straight street hustler to turn gay. More common, though, is when a street hustler becomes monetarily and especially emotionally dependent on one man who is nicer to him than anyone else he knows.

Felix Melendez was the classic street hustler, John Knight the classic john. Though opposites on the socioeconomic scale, they shared the same patriarchal oppression. And little by little, Felix had fallen in love with his John.

Camden County jail. Joe Paolucci's lawyer has talked with his client and Paolucci has agreed to allow me to interview him.

Paolucci is a dark-complexioned, muscular, stocky man. His chest looks as if it's about to bust out of its shirt. His shoulders look as if he's made a career of digging ditches instead of rolling pastry dough at the Italian bakery shop where he worked in South Philadelphia. Frequently, he squeezes his hands in isometric exercises. His wrists are thicker than my calves. A curl drops down his forehead. Paolucci's in the Camden County jail charged with manslaughter. He admitted that, during the course of a criminal endeavor, his former roommate was killed, but specifically denied knowing that Felix Melendez was going to be executed.

The Camden jail is close to the Trailways bus terminal, and visiting quarters are not the kind we've seen in *Each Dawn I Die*. No glass partitions separate prisoner from visitor. Though it isn't the reception salon at Elizabeth Arden, the social quarters are compact and clean, like an optometrist's waiting room. If one wanted to present a favorite convict with a devil's food cake complete with baked-in hacksaw, one probably could. However, a security guard stands on duty outside the cubbyhole where I sit with Paolucci and his lawyer.

I ask Paolucci to begin by explaining how he originally met Felix Melendez.

"I knew Felix from a friend of mine, an older guy who works as a dry cleaner. You see, my wife and I had just separated and I needed a roommate to help pay the bills. So I asked Felix if he'd move in. Altogether, he lived at my house for about seven months.

"In the beginning he was working and going to school. Then he quit everything and got lazy and smoked a lot of grass. During the late summer, he began going down to Center City. I used to lecture him. I told him not to hang out there. I knew he'd get in trouble. But I could have been speaking to a deaf man. Almost every day, he'd split to Spruce and Fifteenth Street, that homosexual area. Felix would always get decked out, all cleaned up, perfumed with that fucking cologne shit on him like he was going to meet Miss Universe."

"Did he make it clear to you that he was hustling gay guys?"

Paolucci's response is quick. "He didn't boast about it, but I knew what he was doing because I went to town a couple of times and saw him at that corner. Definitely, he was selling it. In fact, a couple of times, he phones me to meet him at Spruce. I warned him, 'Man, you'll end up in jail, play it cool.' Do you know that a couple of months before the Knight business, the cops picked Felix up and let him go? They caught him with a knife, but didn't charge him.

"He met John in that neighborhood. I first heard about this rich guy from Felix maybe in September. Then the telephone calls started. I never talked to John in person, only by phone. He'd call the house five or six times a week. If Felix wasn't home, he'd say, 'Tell him John phoned.' He'd never leave his last name.

"One night, they were on the phone with each other two hours. It got me fucking angry. I said to Felix, 'Look, man. I don't mind you using the phone, but two hours of that goddamn shit is too much.'

"A lot of times, they'd argue. I'd hear Felix say, 'Go screw yourself, John,' then he'd hang up. He'd feel real bad after, and mope around, and in ten minutes he'd call him back. It was like they had a romance going.

"Meanwhile, Felix wasn't working and had no money coming in. I told him he's gotta find someplace else to live. Then John started helping him out. Felix suddenly had money and some new flashy clothes.

"The day before John was murdered, those two were on the phone for a long time. No, I don't know what they were talking about."

Paolucci's lawyer sits at the edge of his seat, his legs crossing and uncrossing. We have to be careful here that not too much is said, in case an appeal is made. Might hurt parole. My casette recorder is picking up everything. That I have the machine in jail is not illegal, but the idea is to make its appearance inconspicuous to the guard at the door and not to allow Paolucci to be conscious of its ominous power even though he has agreed to its use. The Sony is on the lap of Paolucci's lawyer, alongside his attaché case.

I ask Paolucci if Felix fucked with other men after he had started "dating" John.

"There was one older guy who kept lecturing him," he answers, gnawing at his cuticles. "This guy would come over to the house and say, 'Felix, I don't want you going to town.' They had a fistfight. Certainly there was something between those two.

"Most of the time, though, Felix had girls coming to the house. He saw this chick, Donna Leone, the one who had his baby. She was over a few times."

"Was he in love with Donna?"

"I don't know. I used to get angry because he'd hit her. I said, 'Don't beat her up, Felix, don't punch her out around here, man. I'm trying to be nice to you. Beating that broad causes a lot of problems. It's embarrassing.'

"Donna was a sore spot. He'd say he loved her and was going to marry her, then he'd say he didn't love her. They were always fighting."

Though he's rocky in stature, there's something soft about Paolucci. His manner is more that of a follower than a leader, a giver more than a taker. His speech is spotted with "dese" and "dose." His voice is low, sometimes inaudible. As he speaks, he avoids eye contact. Whether it's shyness or preoccupation with what's going on inside his own cerebrum, I don't know.

Paolucci was born in Jersey City, attended public school to the sixth grade, shuffled from foster home to foster home, and spent time in prison. His jail record shows that he was first arrested in 1965 on a burglary and larceny charge. In certain ways, his criminal record parallels Salvatore Soli's: car theft, disorderly conduct, shoplifting, threatening someone with violence. It differs in that Paolucci was once picket up on a sodomy charge.

"The cop who made the arrest had a personal grudge against me," he says. "I was taking out his girl. He knew that I wasn't working and was bumming around, so he tried to get me for something embarrassing. Out of spite, he locked me up for sodomy, man. The case was thrown out."

"When you were young, did you play the gay scene?"

"Hey, I'm strictly for broads. But I used to roll the faggots. I didn't screw with them any: just robbed them. A bunch of us would hang out downtown where Felix used to go. We'd lure these guys to the subway. Then we'd punch them out and take their money."

I count to ten, grit my teeth, but keep my mouth shut, afraid that anything I say will bring on an attack of reticence from Paolucci. Some other time, if there is another time.

Paolucci looks at his shoes. The rose tattoo on his arms sways in rhythm to the isometric exercises he does with his fist. "I liked Felix. He was a good guy," he says softly. "I feel bad that it happened."

"Why did Felix get you all involved that night?"

"Why? Because all of a sudden he wanted to be a tough guy. He was feeling blue, I think, because of John. He had never shot up with meth before. Man, that meth does things to your brain cells.

"When Felix and Sal and Steve said they were going to John's apartment, I didn't want to have nothing to do with it. I know that when they got to John's place, Felix told John that the two men he was with were from the Mafia. He warned John to keep his mouth shut."

"Did Felix actually say that he killed Knight?"

"When he came back to the house the morning after, I went downstairs and I saw him and said, 'Man, what happened?' and he answered, 'I had to cut the guy.' He looked real nervous, like he had the shakes. When he said, 'I had to cut the guy,' he made a gesture, like he had knifed him. He had a real big knife on him, a bowie knife, fastened to his leg. He said he got it from Knight's place. And he was wearing jewelry, a lot of good jewelry, which he said he had taken from John's apartment. I warned him. 'Don't come here with that shit, man. Get rid of it.' So he went out and dropped most of the stuff in a nearby sewer.''

"Then he *did* say he knifed Knight?"

"He said he had to cut the guy," repeats Paolucci.

"Did he say why?"

"No."

"This is a crazy question, Joe, but do you think Felix was in love with John Knight?"

Long pause. Eyes on shoes. "Possibly," says Joe Paolucci. He shakes his head. "Possibly. I think yes."

Experience has taught me that newsmen—no matter how important their positions, no matter how tough their current situation—are usually receptive to talking to other members of the press. Call it compassion from having been in the other fellow's shoes. Call it professional understanding. It is nevertheless a fact that William Randolph Hearst was more accessible in his time than Douglas Fairbanks. The Sulzberger family of the *New York Times*, Clay Felker, Rupert Murdoch, Jann Wenner are good copy, whether downing spritzers at Elaine's or discussing tradition or trends or mergers within their respective empires. Rival papers and magazines constantly run stories on newspaper tycoons.

John Shively Knight, the grand old man of journalism, however, was another ball game. Little had been written. The most extensive piece on him appeared in the *New York Herald Tribune* in November 1960, and that story is by-lined by the chief of Knight's

Washington bureau. Analytical the piece isn't. Nice it
certainly is. Puff runs through the copy like cream
through an eclair ("To those who know and work with
him, John Shively Knight is generously endowed with
warmth and human sympathy"). One telling line reads,
"He has had more than his share of the desolation of
personal tragedy, but has been a tight-lipped stoic
during those periods."

Personal tragedy includes the death of his first wife,
Katherine MacLain, of a brain tumor in 1929—eight
years after their marriage. The death of his oldest son,
John, Jr., in action during the very last days of World
War II (John, Jr., was John S. Knight III's father). An
attack of infantile paralysis which befell his middle son
Landon and left him paralyzed from the waist down.
(Landon is now president of the Portgage Newspaper
Supply Company, part of the Knight organization.) The
death of his youngest son, Frank, also of a brain tumor,
in 1948. The death of his second wife, Beryl, four
months before the death of his grandson.

Newspapermen who have worked for Knight describe
him as closemouthed, well-dressed, defiant and aggressive. Vigorous and athletic, he works out with a set
of barbells each morning and rides his bicycle for a
couple of miles near his house in Akron, where he lives
most of the year. When it comes to sex, John Shively
Knight is puritanical.

Yet Earl Wilson remembers Knight as a "tough
cookie" and a "playboy." Wilson worked for him in
1935, covering the state legislature in Ohio for the
Akron Beacon Journal, the first newspaper in the
Knight chain. Years later, Knight asked Wilson if he'd
return to the *Journal* as an editor. Wilson by then had
had a whiff of Broadway, liked the smell, and declined
the offer. (Wilson's Broadway column now runs in the
Philadelphia News.)

Editors and writers on all the Knight-Ridder papers have substantial freedom. The two things Knight insists on are reportage that tells both sides of the story and writing that produces short sentences. His column, "The Editor's Notebook," appeared in his papers off and on for years. Though generally conservative in tone, many of his columns argued against United States involvement in Vietnam. In 1960, he claimed, "I'm going to vote for Nixon and will probably support him. I like Nixon, but I must say he hasn't fired me up very much."

What did ignite Knight was a series of articles in the *Detroit Free Press* condemning conditions at the Wayne County Jail. The articles were supervised by John Knight III and led to a prison cleanup. Grandpa burst his buttons with pride: it was chip-off-the-old-block time.

Through the years, stories have been written comparing John Shively Knight with Joseph Kennedy. Though tragedy followed Knight the way tire tracks follow a Cadillac down a muddy road, durability is his middle name. Still, he carries an eraser in his head, and can obliterate the past at will. But first he has to know it all.

Newsmen who attended young John's funeral in Columbus, Georgia, claim the old man was both inquisitive and easy to talk with.

With accessibility in mind, I decide to phone him. Knight has just returned to his office at the *Akron Beacon Journal*, and getting through to him is easy. A secretary answers the phone and suggests that I tell her what the call is about. "He's busy now," she says. "I'll tell him."

An hour later, Knight phones back. His opening words are, "I'm gun-shy.

"I've talked to *Newsweek* and *Time* and have been

misquoted,'' he continues. ''To discuss my relationship with my grandson is still painful.''

Nevertheless, he states that young John was an excellent newsman. ''No doubt about that.'' And that he knows his grandson was liked both personally and professionally. Had he lived, his career would have been a brilliant one.

''We had a close relationship, John and I—a close and warm relationship. We understood each other and were on the best of terms. There were no differences. Never any differences. And I have no self-recrimination about any of what has happened.

''After John's death, I spent three days in solitude at Massachusetts General Hospital thinking over every aspect of his life as it applied to me. There is nothing that I would have done differently. No changes I'd have made.''

I ask if he'd see me, if only to reminisce about his grandson's life, as opposed to the circumstances surrounding his death.

''Reviewing our relationship would be very painful,'' he repeats. ''I'm afraid not.''

Several weeks later, John Shively Knight, at age eighty-one, marries for the third time. His wife, Elizabeth Good Augustus, age seventy-four, is a breeder of thoroughbred horses. She has been living in Waite Hill, a Cleveland suburb, and is the widow of a Cleveland millionaire who had been a president of the National Council of the Boy Scouts.

In the late spring of 1976, I phone John S. Knight again. And, once again, he refuses to be interviewed. However, he speculates that John III would have been pleased about his new marriage. ''He and Mrs. Augustus met at a Thanksgiving luncheon in Waite Hill last year. They got along famously.

''While we're talking,'' he continues, ''let me

reiterate that stories about my late grandson's wealth are greatly exaggerated. Officially, he was not the heir. That had been reported erroneously. John held some stock which I gave to him, but we're a corporation and a man has to earn his own way in the business."

Whether or not John was the heir apparent, his grandfather was in a position to bestow upon him the title of heir positive. John Shively Knight controlled two million shares of the Knight newspapers, or better than 35 percent of the outstanding common stock. A good portion of that stock was slated to go to John S. Knight III.

Each Christmas, young John would receive several hundred shares in his stocking. Just before he left Philadelphia, his grandfather rewrote his will establishing a trust that would keep the newspaper stock intact, but would give his heir voting power over the trust. Less than a year before John's death, he was given 35,000 shares. The gift amounted to between $900,000 and one million dollars. Grandpa paid the gift tax.

Despite Grandpa's protest, unofficially there was never any doubt that John was the heir or that he was being groomed as the next Citizen Knight. Had his abilities swayed toward the business end of journalism, he'd have been shipped off to Miami, because the *Miami Herald* is the best school for learning the corporate aspects of journalism. Since signs of printer's ink flowed through his veins, the master plan was to send young John to Detroit after his graduation from Harvard. There, the corporation could find out if he was a good reporter. At the *Detroit Free Press*, he'd have to produce. He could also learn the ropes, from paper routing to advertising. Once schooled, he would be transferred to Philadelphia, where the two Knight-Ridder papers are the best training grounds for an executive editor or would-be publisher.

Acquaintances who know both Johns claim that the

family ties are extraordinarily strong. Grandfather
Knight took the role of daddy almost from the moment
John was born, leaving his mother a sort of subordinate
figure who went along with decisions regarding the
master plan. Grandfather was responsible for sending
John away from home to school when he was
moderately young, for putting the bug in his ear about
Oxford and Harvard.

A pessimist would think that the burden of tradition
would drive a kid up a wall, but John III adored,
coddled, and feared his grandfather. "He genuflected
each time he talked about the old man," says a
newspaper chum, "but I think he had a deep
penetrating anger and hate toward him. He was
desperately afraid of his grandfather. He was afraid of
doing wrong, afraid of his wrath and displeasure."
Patricide was the name of the game. Or, to be more
exact, grandpatricide.

"When John lived in Detroit, he bought a Picasso
lithograph to give to his grandpa for his birthday,"
remembers the newsman. "He might have been twenty-
five years old then, but he trembled, afraid that the old
man might think he hadn't spent enough money.

"Face it. He didn't want to alienate his grandfather.
He wanted to inherit the works. John wanted to run the
newspaper chain."

Apparently he didn't consider catering a form of
whoring. It was more a matter of being realistic. One
form of catering was to pretend to share his grandfather's love of horse racing. John made it his business
to follow the Kentucky Derby. On at least two occasions, he called his grandfather and placed bets with
him. John deliberately did not select the horse he
thought would win. Instead, he'd bet against his grandfather's favorite indiscriminately, in order to lose.

Often the two would spend New Year's Day together

watching the Rose Bowl game, drinking, and discussing life. Just enough information was fed to his grandfather—no more, no less—to keep the patriarch aware of John's wanderings, his interests, and his progress. Hardly any information was given about his insecurities.

Ironically, most people who know John Shively Knight claim he would not have been vindictive had John III confessed his homosexual feelings. If young John had a reasonable adult relationship with another man, it's unlikely that grandfather would have hit the ceiling. But John was fucking with street kids. Boy or girl kids, the situation was a flammable one. Too much was at stake. A scandal of the chicken-hawk sort could affect the corporation and John III's future role in the empire. No way would Granddad approve.

Pretty well in the background during the days and weeks following the tragedy lurks John's mother, Dorothy. Not exactly a black sheep, certainly not one of the family, Dorothy Knight was considered a social inferior almost from the first day she was introduced to the man who was to be her father-in-law.

First of all, her background wasn't wealth: the former Dorothy Wells's father sold used cars. Secondly, her romance with the newspaper czar's son budded during the war years, when Johnny Doughboy married the prettiest, sweetest girl on the home front before he went off to serve Uncle Sam.

Dorothy's husband was Johnny Doughboy. They met while he was stationed at Fort Benning near Columbus, fell in love, and married. Their honeymoon was short. During the last days of the war, Lieutenant John Knight, Jr., age twenty-two, got himself killed in combat at Hullern, Germany. Great measures were taken to keep his death a secret from his very pregnant wife. John Shively Knight ordered the Columbus paper and radio station to hold the announcement. Two weeks after John, Jr.'s death, John Knight III was born. The date was April 13, 1945. Dorothy Knight found out about her husband's demise a few days after the child's birth.

Grandfather Knight helped support Dorothy and her baby. From the beginning, he was Santa Claus to the kid. To his widowed daughter-in-law, he continued to be courteous, yet distant. Neither forced courtesy nor spoiling her child endeared John Shively Knight to Dorothy.

But Dorothy and the child were close. All through young John's formative years, the two were snug as a bug in a rug, chums, buddies. After all, Mother was playing surrogate father, too. The relationship changed when John was sent away at age fifteen by Grandpa to exclusive Lawrenceville School in New Jersey. Here, for the first time, the young man had friends his own age. And he bloomed. Suddenly he was the quintessential preppie—editing the school literary magazine, excelling in sports, dabbling in student theater.

At Lawrenceville, John told a buddy that he and his mother didn't agree on some basic philosophical things, such as life in general, and that he was always irritated because Mother didn't like to travel and seldom left Columbus.

There were several reasons why Dorothy Knight preferred staying at home. She suffered from pleurisy. She was a full-time working woman: her profession was selling real estate for Rust and Malloy. And if her son insisted that she visit her in-laws in Akron, that was a particular problem. Not only was she uncomfortable with her father-in-law, she actually disliked John Sr.'s second wife.

During his college years, however, John III continued to visit his mother, although sporadically. When he worked in Detroit, the visits were even less frequent. In Columbus, Dorothy Knight lived modestly, never beyond her working means. When John visited Georgia, life there was decidedly different from the old-style grandeur of his grandfather's house in Akron. He preferred the life-style of Akron.

Until the day of her son's funeral, Dorothy Knight was kept ignorant of his double life and the grisly particulars of his death. The *Columbus Enquirer* and *Columbus Ledger*—both Knight-Ridder newspapers —deliberately avoided details for the first four days following his killing. On the day of the funeral, they broke the story in full. That same day, Dorothy Knight's minister sat with her and discussed the circumstances of the murder. Mrs. Knight was shocked and shaken.

At the funeral, she had to be held up. She cried a steady stream of tears. There was no way that she could accept her loss. Executives of the Knight-Ridder empire kept people away from her who wanted to question her about her son. And they still do. John Knight's mother has always stayed in the background. Dorothy Knight is considered a recluse in Columbus.

As next of kin, she inherited all his possessions: the stocks, the bank account, the artwork, the furniture in Rittenhouse Square.

Fate plays funny tricks indeed.

December 14. They've seized Salvatore Soli in Miami. I think if I were Salvatore Soli, I'd flee to Miami, too. The weather is chilly in Philly. Frigid. I read Soli's story and decide to call my parents at their condominium near Palm Beach. They beg me to visit them, get a little sunburn, swim in the pool. They want to know what I'm up to. I ask if there has been anything about Soli's capture in the Florida papers. My father tells me he's heard about the *tsimmes*. He suggests that I move from my dump in Manhattan. If I can't afford the rent in a good high-rise, he'll help me out.

Parents, commitments, obligations, umbilical cords that are tough to sever even after the grown son leaves home. Do orphans and bastards have it easier?

Soli, with all of his philandering, with his arrest record and track marks, was still closer to his mother than Camden is to Philly. Mama Soli would call her son every day, no matter where he was. He hadn't called since the Knight murder. What could be more natural than for Antoinette Soli to go on television and plead, "Salvi, please come home or get in touch with me. Let me know you're all right. You may be dead like that boy Felix Melendez."

Through the magic of the media, Mrs. Soli reminds her son that she is critically ill, having suffered a massive heart attack less than a year before. "The operation was unsuccessful," she weeps. "They don't expect me to live more than a year."

At Chock Full o' Nuts, where I wait for the florist to meet me, Mrs. Soli's anguished face leaps out from the pages of the *News*. A hooker on the next stool reads the article with relish.

"He should be in a mental institution," she says to the counterwoman. "The aggravation he's giving his poor mother."

She puts down her *News*. "I wonder if they're giving a reward?" she says to no one in particular. She orders another coffee. "Light."

Two of her cohorts enter the place. One is a Katy Jurado look-alike who glances at Soli's picture.

"He looks familiar. Cute," she says.

"Just caught," says the first hooker. "I think they're giving a reward."

"Forget the reward. I'd do it with him for nothing. Wouldn't you?" She looks at me.

"No," I answer. "Not for nothing." I make a mental note to check the mirror to see if my skin has turned lavender.

There's no reward. Soli was turned in by Linda Mary Wells, an eighteen-year-old "burlesque dancer" who ratted to protect herself. She told detectives she was with Soli in Philadelphia early on the night that John Knight was murdered.

The scenario of events immediately preceding and following the killing reads like the screenplay of a James M. Cain novel. It begins when Linda Mary Wells arrived in Philadelphia early in November from Syracuse, where she had run away from home. Linda is a honey blonde with a pug nose, a movie-starlet figure, vague but sweet; like a dandelion caught in a maelstrom, yet determined to survive. Definitely not clerk-typist material.

Within a few days after Linda's arrival, she had found employment at a Center City burlesque theater called the Troc. There she adopted the name Tarri and took off her clothes nightly in a very refined manner. She also hooked up with a pint-sized Mickey Rooney drug dealer named Salvatore Soli, a punk well known in South Philly for his volatile temper, his skirmishes with the law, his loyalty to his family, and especially his way with the broads.

Linda had known Sal only a few days when he invited her—along with another blonde named Donna DePaul—to a friend's house for a Saturday night of "doing drugs." The friend was also an ex-con, a guy Sal Soli had met in prison seven years before. Joe Paolucci was his name, and he had this two-story house in South

Philly where Sal would stay, on and off. Sort of a second home.

To Soli, Linda was just another momentary diversion in his life. To Linda, Sal was a temporary stopping point on the road to a show biz career. Besides which, that other blonde, Donna, was his girl. But it was a Saturday: Sal promised he had some interesting friends, some interesting drugs, so why not make a night of it?

About 11 P.M., Linda and Sal and Donna and Joe were lounging around the downstairs living room, drinking beer and watching TV, when acquaintances dropped by. First, Stevie Maleno came over to cop some drugs from Sal. That wasn't unusual, because Stevie was an addict who got drugs from Sal at least once or twice a week. Soon after, Felix Melendez sauntered in. Felix was Joe's roommate. Felix had never met anybody in the room before, except, of course, for Joe.

For some odd reason, Felix was discombobulated, as if his body were in the room but his head in Jupiter. He flopped in a corner, out of it. Then moved to the table, where the others were sitting, to partake of the dynamite grass that was being pased around.

Reality, such as it is, is easier to cope with when one is high. Realistically, Felix volunteered, "I should be somewhere else." To get him somewhere else, he shot up with the meth that Salvatore Soli offered.

In fact, everyone shot up, except Joe Paolucci.

As expected, Felix was soon floating—jetting in his own space. Then the talk turned to drugs and money. Salvatore remarked that he was in need of quick bucks and the girls said they'd they'd like to get off on LSD. Felix instantly left his private world. He declared he had a rich friend they could rip off. The offer was made spontaneously, as if the drugs and surrounding conversation were preludes to the theme of the evening: rip off the rich friend.

"Who is he?" asked Salvatore.

"John Knight."

"Call him," demanded Sal.

Felix obeyed. He promenaded to the far corner of the room, dialed John Knight's number, waited three rings. Everyone in the room, meanwhile, had hushed.

When Knight answered, Felix said "John, I've got to see you. Can I come over?" Pause. Then Felix said "I've got to, John. It's urgent." Long wait. Then, "Okay, I won't come over until your friends leave." He hung up and explained that Knight had guests from out of town, and couldn't see him now.

Soli refused to let it ride. "Call him again."

About 2:30 A.M., Felix went upstairs. He showered and got all dolled up. Linda Wells thought he had doused himself in Skinny Dip, "a woman's perfume." She thought he looked like a flaming faggot, the way he was dressed: feminine, yet masculine. Too fancy for her tastes.

In his Superfly drag, Felix dialed Knight, again. This time, he swung the phone into the hallway, taking the extension wire as far as it could reach so that Knight wouldn't hear Sal, who was instructing Felix what to say, and Linda and Donna, who were laughing at him.

Felix said, "John I love you." He said it in a high voice, the voice of a stereotypical gay man—or possibly the voice of a drugged man who was desperate and hysterical.

"I love you," Felix repeated. He said it loud enough so that everyone in the room could hear. And everyone laughed. Nevertheless, Felix continued his plea. "I need to be with you, John. Yes, I'll see you after your friends leave. I love you, John. I love you."

Minutes later, Felix Melendez left the house, accompanied by Salvatore Soli and Steve Maleno. Sal had a .32 pistol in his coat pocket. They took Sal's Mercury and drove to the Dorchester Apartments.

During the three and a half hours that they were gone, Joe, Donna, and Linda continued to smoke grass. They played cards. For a short while, Joe and Linda abandoned Donna. They disappeared upstairs to Joe's bedroom and fucked.

At 7 A.M., the phone rang. Donna answered. It was Sal. "Tell Joe to get his car and pick us up," he said in a frantic voice. "We're in trouble. You come along, too." He gave Donna instructions as to where he and Steve Maleno would be. Immediately, Donna and Joe left the house and drove to the designated corner.

"What the hell happened?" demanded Joe Paolucci. "What went wrong? Where's Felix?"

Sal spat out that they were in a lot of trouble. "Felix went amuck," he said. "He cut up the guy."

Sal gave Donna his car keys and told her to pick up his Mercury near Rittenhouse Square, then he and Steve hopped into Joe's Caddy. Once back at Joe's house, Sal dumped the cache from John Knight's apartment on the kitchen table: gold coins, credit cards, checkbooks with the name McKinnon printed on them, jewelry, articles engraved with the initials JSK. He was like a panther, ready to pounce. "The kid went berserk," he muttered repeatedly. Steve Maleno was calm, though: tranquil, as if nothing had happened, and casually examined the new collection of valuables. Fine that they had ripped off some of the dude's shit, he thought, but too bad that the faggot didn't have any drugs at his pad.

Linda, who had remained at the house all along, noticed that Steve had blood on his arms, his jacket, shoes, and pants leg; and that Sal had blood on his shoes. She helped Steve wipe off the blood. Steve told her that they had left Felix behind to make sure that nobody followed them. He also told her that there was another couple at the apartment, but nothing was said or known at the time about Felix stabbing Rosemary McKinnon.

When Donna returned to the house—the car parked outside—Sal put together a battle plan. The cops would be after them. They'd have to split from Philadelphia immediately. He told Joe Paolucci to hang around, though, so that at least one of them would be there when Felix came back to the house. He told Stevie and Donna to start packing. He himself piled the loot into a couple of paper bags. And when they were all set to leave, he asked Linda to tag along, almost as an afterthought. On meth, one is easily accessible to suggestions. Linda agreed to be the extra baggage on the trip.

At 9 A.M. Sunday, they checked into the Bo-Bet Motel in Mount Ephraim, New Jersey. Donna registered; they were given a two-room suite. Then the quartet parked themselves in the living room with its convertible sofa bed, lamps that looked like stuffed munchkins, faded prints of American landscapes, and a radiator that hissed. They turned on the radio. The regular Sunday-morning religious program was abruptly interrupted for a news report:

"John Knight, newspaper heir and editor at the Philadelphia *News*, was stabbed to death at his Rittenhouse Square apartment early this morning. The victim's luxury apartment had been ransacked and the identity of his murderer—or murderers—is unknown."

The radio announcer discussed the findings abstractly, as if the victim were an actor in a film. Sal listened, talked back to the radio, and seethed. His world had fallen apart overnight. To calm himself, he shot up with meth. Linda and Donna shot up, too. Steve declined. He was only vaguely aware of the seriousness of the night's events. Exhausted, he fell into a deep sleep on the couch.

As Stevie slept, Sal proceeded to tear up and burn bankbooks and credit cards—anything from Knight's apartment that wasn't negotiable. He flushed the cinders down the toilet.

Around 1 P.M., he told Donna to call Joe Paolucci.

"Get him to haul his ass down here, and to bring Felix."

A couple of hours later, the roommates showed at the motel. Joe was puzzled by the turn of events and kept his mouth shut. Whether it was remorse stemming from Knight's death or fear of what was to come, Felix appeared stupefied. However, Sal would not leave him alone.

"Why did you kill John Knight? Why the Christ did you kill him?"

Sal wouldn't stop.

"Look what you got us into. You didn't have to kill that guy. Why'dja have to kill him? I ought to kill you now."

To intensify matters, the radio newscaster suddenly reported that Rosemary McKinnon, too, had been stabbed.

"What?" yelled Sal. He leaped on top of Felix and started strangling him. Joe Paolucci pulled Sal off.

"Did you stab that broad? You did, didn't you? What the fuck happened?"

Felix was panic-stricken. He had just told Sal that he knew nothing. He had tried to act cool. But he was like a schoolboy caught by his teacher in a lie. The way out was to fess up.

"She tried to escape," Felix explained. "I was leaving John's apartment and she was in the hall, hollering. She grabbed me. I stabbed her. I was scared."

"Don't tell us lies," screamed Steve Maleno, who was abruptly wide awake. "Tell us the truth. What happened? Why did you stab that woman?"

Felix rasped, "I'm telling the truth. I stabbed her in the elevator and cut her hand. It wasn't like I was trying to kill her. I was scared. That's the truth."

Steve and Sal continued to interrogate. They battered Felix with queries and accusations and refused to accept any of his answers.

Finally, they stopped. Witnessing the violence was too much for Linda. She ran to the bathroom and showered. She scrubbed her flesh until it was almost raw, as if to cleanse herself of the ugliness that had invaded her life. She continued to take showers: three, four, five that day; several the following day.

Donna kept calm. Eventually, Donna left the motel with Steve Maleno, who had chopped up a couple of bars of soap, called a couple of drug contacts in Philadelphia, and advised them that he had meth to sell. For this particular transaction, Stevie took along a gun, figuring that if his buyers spotted the meth for soap and put up a stink, he'd just have to take their money by force.

Sal, Joe, and Felix left the motel, too, leaving Linda alone with her showers. They dropped in on one of Sal's contacts and tried to scare up some ready cash which would see them through the next few days.

Combinations constantly changed during the early evening hours. Donna and Steve Maleno went out for chicken. Donna went with Sal to visit his lawyer for advice.

While Sal and Donna were gone, Steve Maleno resumed his blitzkrieg attack on Felix. He bombarded him with new accusations, threatened to kill him, then took a butcher knife and sliced a hole in his head. Blood gushed. Linda ran to the bathroom and gathered a few towels, which she administered to Felix. Nevertheless, blood trickled down his face, onto his coat, onto the couch. But Felix kept quiet, fearing that the slightest provocation would start Maleno off again.

When Sal returned to the motel, he and Joe and Steve shut themselves into the kitchenette area. "What are we going to do about Felix?" demanded Steve. "We can't trust him. He knows too much. What should we do? Leave the country? Leave the state? Keep running?"

The men decided that the logical next stage of their flight would be to leave the Bo-Bet. But first they watched the 11 P.M. television newscast. Though not named, Soli, Melendez, and Maleno were described, down to the track marks on Soli's arms, courtesy of Rosemary McKinnon's amazing memory. It was another twinge of pain in the ongoing nightmare for all of them.

Toward midnight, they separated into two cars. Steve and Felix got into Joe's white and brown '65 Cadillac. Sal and the two women got into Sal's '68 Mercury Montego. Both vehicles circled the Jersey countryside for close to an hour. Linda was confused as to where they were heading. Sal consoled her with, "We're taking Felix to his uncle's house."

At a fork in the road, Sal stopped his car and signaled Joe Paolucci to pull over. Steve Maleno got out of Paolucci's car, entered Sal's for a minute or two. Linda saw Sal hand Stevie a gun. She heard Sal say, "Keep it quiet."

The cars started up again. Eventually, they stopped at a dead end. Joe parked his Caddy behind Sal's auto. Both vehicles turned off their lights. Steve told Joe, "We gotta bury this shit." He and Felix got out of Joe's car. They headed toward a wooded area. Steve carried a bag containing coats, dungarees, shirts and shoes that they had worn when they ripped off Knight's apartment, as well as blood-soaked towels from the Bo-Bet. Both he and Felix began digging a hole in which to dispose of the stuff. But Steve started again. "Why did you kill that man?"

He pulled the gun from the waist of his pants. And fired point blank at Felix's face. Felix fell. Leaning over him, Steve fired two more shots.

Hurriedly, he took the bag with the garments and returned to Joe Paolucci's car. Less than a mile away, he dumped the clothing in a suburban garbage can. Then he dismantled the gun and, piece by piece, tossed it out the car window. Particles of the weapon became part of the New Jersey landscape.

Linda Mary Wells had heard the shots. "Be calm," she told herself. "Play it dumb." So with Sal beside her at the wheel, she pretended she didn't hear anything and chattered on like an animated chipmunk. But she had seen Steve return to Joe's car alone and knew that he had taken care of Felix. She realized also that she knew too much and that she might be taken care of next.

Sal started up the car and continued down the highway, with Joe's car following. To make matters worse, Sal's muffler was acting up—he was afraid the noise might draw attention from highway police—so both vehicles headed toward Moe's Sunoco gas station on the Blackhorse Turnpike.

As the service station attendant worked on the muffler and refueled the tanks, Linda wandered over to Steve and nonchalantly asked him if he had gotten Felix to his uncle's house okay.

"Yeah," he replied.

"Good," said Linda, who had inevitably relegated herself to the role of the good-natured wisecracking easygoing blonde of the company, in contrast to Donna's serious but tough peroxided moll. In her Judy Holliday capacity, Linda made a couple of silly jokes to Steve, but her sense of humor was not applauded. Later, Linda was to remember, "My mind was very—not there."

Just before the group resumed their journey, Steve took Linda aside.

"You didn't see anything," he whispered, "so you don't know for a fact if anything happened. All you know is that Felix is at his uncle's."

Linda nodded. But racing through her mind was the thought that Felix was killed because he was dangerous. "Felix kept saying things that he didn't do, but it turned out he did. They asked him in the motel why he killed John Knight and he said 'Just because.' They murdered Felix because they felt that they were patsies, set up for Felix's lovers' quarrel. Felix wanted to have them there to help him in his fight with Knight." If Steve could kill Felix in cold blood, would she be next?

The threat of impending doom rode with Linda during the days that followed.

Early Monday morning, the group checked into the Monticello Motel off the turnpike, and went to sleep for the remainder of the dark. Sal and Donna shared one bed. Linda slept with Joe Paolucci. Steve slept alone.

At 4:30 P.M. on Monday, December 8, they registered at the Bellemawr Motor Inn in Bellemawr, New Jersey. Later that evening, Steve announced that he had business in Philadelphia. He told Sal that he had to borrow his car. Sal balked. In so many words, he ordered Stevie to stay put. Sal figured that if they were all together, there'd be less of a chance of one of them getting picked up and squealing on the others. But Steve was determined to see his wife and his mother and to do a little more drug dealing. Despite Sal's dire warnings, he was off to Philly, whether Sal liked it or not. Sal gave Steve his car keys. Linda decided to go along with Steve.

They stopped at Apple's Corner, a restaurant populated mostly by blacks. Steve transacted a deal with a pusher. Then he and Linda motored to South Philadelphia to visit Steve's estranged wife. Linda chose to remain in the car. She observed the Malenos carrying on a heated conversation.

Steve was out of sorts when they drove to the opposite side of Philly to visit his parents. He told his mother about the events of the past few days and assured her that everything would be all right. Nevertheless, Steve cautioned his mother to keep her mouth shut, just in case—no telling what might happen.

Next stop was a Center City drugstore, where Steve and Linda picked up a few packages of hair coloring. One was blond, another ultra-blue, another a light brown. Linda also bought a couple of combs and a hairbrush. If only she had a prescription for Valium: her heart was in her mouth. "I didn't know whether somebody was watching me from afar, whether I was about to get arrested."

When they returned from their excursion, Steve whispered to Sal that he wanted to kill Linda. Then he made an offhand comment that he also wanted to rub out Donna and Joe Paolucci. Having bumped off Felix, Steve was into the TV thing—the whole Baretta, Starsky and Hutch thing. He felt he had to kill everybody.

It wasn't right, Sal reasoned to himself. Felix was one thing, but not the girls. The correct move would be to get away from his gun-happy confrere in crime. When the opportune moment arose, he'd flee with Linda and Donna to Miami.

Right then, however, the moment was ripe for a little amateur beauty work. Donna got out the dye pot. She streaked her hair blue, dyed Sal's a reddish blond, and tinkered with Steve's until it metamorphosed into a jet black far darker than his natural color.

In their snazzy new disguises, Donna and Steve—along with Linda—ventured across the street to the local bar and grill. Steve and Donna ordered gin and tonics. Linda sipped a Seven-Up.

Five sips down, she noticed that a police car was cruising the parking lot outside. A spotlight flashed into the restaurant. Panic.

Quickly, Steve split to the men's room. He dawdled there, expecting disaster to break in with a machine gun.

On top of the commode, he spotted a Philadelphia newspaper. What immediately caught his eye was an artist's sketch of himself, Sal, and Felix. The paper offered no identification, but the likenesses were strong.

Steve tucked his shirt back into his pants, crumbled up the paper, flushed the toilet, strolled back to the counter, and ordered Linda and Donna to finish their drinks. The cop who had shined the spotlight sat on a stool next to Linda. She smiled at him as she got up leave. Her smile was both flirtatious and innocent, enough to charm the birds off the trees.

The trio returned to the motel and listened to news reports for most of the rest of the night. Details of the Knight murder continued to flood the airwaves. Police expected a break in the case within the next twenty-four hours.

On Tuesday, December 9, Steve drove to South Philadelphia again, this time without Linda, and returned to the motel with his estranged wife. It was a short visit—about thirty minutes. He took his wife back to South Philadelphia.

The next time Steve returned to his comrades, they weren't there. Two nights later, he gave himself up.

It seems that Sal had decided that the time was ripe for a move south—without Steve. On Wednesday, he, Donna, and Linda got into his Montego and hit the turnpike.

Their first stop was somewhere in Delaware. Endless hours at a garage: the car had broken down and needed major adjustments. Then a stop at a motel between Baltimore and Washington. It was getting to the point where every room looked the same. Linda was ready to scream. This was not what she had left Syracuse and Mama for.

The game of hop, skip, and jump continued. A stop at a motel in Virginia. On to Florence, South Carolina, where Sal dumped the car in a parking lot. Finally, on Friday night, Linda, Donna, and Sal boarded a Greyhound bus for Miami.

They arrived in the Land of Sunshine at two forty Saturday afternoon, checked their coats and luggage at a bus terminal locker, grabbed a cab, and went shopping at Woolworth's and Lerner's. At a shopping-arcade, jewelry store, Sal was able to unload some of Knight's stolen property. He sold a gold chain, a gold I.D. bracelet, and a gold Queen Elizabeth coin. For the loot, he received $150. The money would tide them over for a while. In fact, there was a new optimism.

Why not? With his short-cropped strawberry-blond hair and minus his moustache, Sal could hardly recognize himself when he looked in the mirror. Surely, he'd be safe at last. Here in Miami, he'd be lost in the shuffle—just another body in the crunch of bronzed vacationers and golden-skinned beachboys who populate the oceanfront cabanas.

He got Donna to check them into the South Winds Motel in Miami. They were exhausted after the long trip. The two women fell into a deep sleep. When Linda awoke, Sal suggested that they get off on meth. Out came the needle and syringe.

As in a muted, pink-cloud Technicolor dream, Sal slowly began to undress Linda. And, in a bed next to the one in which Donna rested, they had anal intercourse. It was their first time fucking together and it was fabulous, with the added kinkiness of Sal's girl friend lying prone within touching distance. "They're all freaks when it comes to sex," Linda later wistfully sighed.

But the freakiness of the week's events continued to gnaw. Linda was more "eerie in the head" than before. Late Sunday afternoon, Sal sent her out to make Xerox copies of a phony birth certificate and social security card. His intention was to change his name and identity completely.

Linda put on a blue blouse and matching slacks. She headed for downtown Miami. For what seemed like hours, she walked around, mulling her predicament. It was her first time alone in a week. The feeling of freedom delighted her. Enough of this being an accessory to the fact and a fugitive.

At Bayfront Park, she spotted a ranger. Linda went right over to him and said, "I've got to talk to someone."

"What's wrong?" he responded.

"I know something about those murders in Philadelphia."

The ranger didn't question her. Instead, he placed a call to the Homicide Division in Miami. Within minutes, a squad car picked up Linda and brought her to headquarters. And before night's end, Sal and Donna were apprehended at the South Winds Motel.

Sal gave up without a struggle. At first, he denied his identity, then later admitted who he was. He refused to admit that he was involved in the Knight slaying. No weapons were found in the room, but cops confiscated narcotics paraphernalia and an ounce of marijuana.

On Monday morning, December 15, several Philadelphia homicide detectives flew to Miami to begin extradition proceedings. Both Linda and Donna were held on narcotics-possession charges stemming from the Florida arrests. Linda's bail was set at $3500, Donna's at $2250. In Philadelphia, warrants were issued charging the women with hindering the apprehension and prosecution of Soli.

At the Dade County, Florida, hearing, Linda appeared dressed in blue jeans and a blue T-shirt with a butterfly design on the chest. Speaking softly, she told the judge, "I'm in burlesque. I have a job in Philadelphia in burlesque."

Two days later, Sal, Linda, and Donna boarded a champagne flight to Philadelphia. The suspects didn't sample the bubbly—when a stewardess offered a glass to Soli, the Philadelphia homicide detective who accompanied him waved her away. After the plane landed, Donna was escorted down the ramp, followed by Linda. When Linda saw the crowd of onlookers and curiosity seekers, she collapsed. She was returned to the plane, then carried down the stairs on a stretcher. An ambulance rushed her to Philadelphia General Hospital, where she was treated for abdominal pains.

In court the following day, Linda told an assistant district attorney that she was feeling "a little bit better." Her parents, she said, would provide an attorney. Bail was set for Linda and Donna at $100,000 each.

Same day, same courtroom, Salvatore Soli stood silently before the judge, his hands shackled behind his back. He was ordered held without bail. Nino Tinari, his lawyer, insisted that Soli be kept in a different jail from Steven Maleno. The judge agreed.

On December 23, an all-day preliminary hearing was held in a City Hall courtroom. Plainclothesmen were everywhere, the security unusually heavy.

Linda looked tired as she testified. She claimed that she saw Soli after he and Maleno returned from Knight's apartment, toting paper bags full of stolen articles. "Sal was upset, nervous, and tensed up. He told me that he 'couldn't believe what happened at the apartment,' that 'the guy Felix just stabbed John.'"

Her testimony also implicated Steven Maleno in the killing of Felix Melendez. "I helped wash blood off

Steve's clothes,'' she confessed. She told reporters that she had ''plenty of nightmares about it. I just want to blank it out, that's all.''

A few weeks later, Linda was back dancing at the Troc. She was a big box office attraction. The manager compared her to the Woman in Red, who turned in John Dillinger in 1934.

This time, she didn't use the name Tarri.

Linda Mary Wells stripped under her own name and who ever heard of Syracuse?

It's two days before Christmas. When I return to the Warwick Hotel after a hearing at City Hall, there's a message from the florist to phone him. He invites me to dinner. We are to be paired off in couples, he says: a doctor and his teeny-bopper friend, a dancer and a hairdresser, a poet and his lawyer-lover, the florist and me.

Holidays are a big deal to him. Christmas cards, Johnny Mathis records, hours spent shopping for presents. His Christmas tree overwhelms the living room, and our relationship—or what is suddenly expected of it—is beginning to overwhelm me.

A relationship is not what I need now. I don't want romance to get in the way of the work that I'm doing. After a day in court, emotional entanglement is the last thing on my mind. I doubt if I'd allow anyone short of Mick Jagger to slow me down at this point.

Once, when questioned by the florist about the *raison d'être* of my work, I didn't have an answer. I didn't want to think about it, or pursue the topic with him.

Not that the florist and I talk much about feelings. We exchange data. My data is far more interesting than his, because what can you say about propagating begonias that hasn't already been said?

Under my florist's roof, I try to play down my involvement in the Knight case. Because each time a burst of enthusiasm erupts, each time I divulge a new delicious morsel to him, I find that he withdraws. And he drinks. Heavily. The drinking was there long before I hit Philadelphia.

Of course, his guests know that I'm a *Voice* reporter from New York covering the hot story in town, and the story is what they want to hear about—from the first glass of *glögg* on. What does it matter that the florist's eggs didn't devil right, or that the crowd at Strawbridge and Clothier's makes shopping impossible? The diners couldn't care less. They want to know if Steve Maleno is a hustler. Is he handsome? Do I think that Felix actually loved John Knight? What kind of pornography did the cops find in Knight's apartment? Dildoes? Tit clamps? Cat-o'-nine-tails? Let's have another drink.

"Let's not talk Knight talk," I offer, shifting the conversation to Judith Exner and the Quinlan case. No dice. Back it comes. The heir and the hustler—that's all they want to hear, through soup, the baby-chicken course, down to cordials.

I begin to chafe at the bit. The florist is too polite to say "Enough, already." Finally, I'm rude to the hairdresser, snippy, actually. A hush falls. Florist swigs down his scotch straight and states, "This is my party. Goddamn it. Drop it, or get the fuck out."

He puts on Christmas music. Loud, then soft. Grass goes round the room. The guests grow mellow and the Knight case drifts away.

As soon as the last couple leaves, we hit the sack. There's an attempt at lovemaking and an embarrassing attempt at soul baring. I discover that the florist's last lover had been a sadist, that the florist had been in a terrible car accident when he was young. The physical scars were removed by plastic surgery. The emotional scars remain.

The talk is tender, the mood sublime, but the

barricade gates inside are constantly on the ready to be closed. To finalize the push, I ask myself—while he's still talking—a question that I dare not ask aloud. Why is it that when a gay man is afraid to tell another that he loves him—afraid that he might be rejected—why is it that he pulls out all the sob-sister negative stuff at his beck and call? Why should gay men have the market on self-pity? Certainly homosexuals don't have the market on unrequited love.

Or am I projecting again? Projecting about something that happened to me a long time ago?

When we awake, the night's revelations aren't discussed. We wash dishes, clean up, sip black coffee, and munch cookies that his mother has sent him for Christmas. The day is crisp and clear—what's left of it—and we walk the Center City streets—down Spruce, around the Dorchester, past the Art Deco antique shops with beaded bags and crystal decanters in the windows, the brass-bed store, the Glass Onion, spots that John Knight frequented less than three weeks ago. We say little to each other. Even when we stop to eat, we say little.

That night, Christmas eve, I take a bus back to New York. Christmas is spent alone.

THE

INTERLUDE

CATCHING UP. Returning phone calls. Stocking my refrigerator. Cutting off leaves that have died on my avocado plants. Flushing a dead goldfish down the toilet. Opening hundreds of pieces of junk mail—screening notices of movies I missed when I was in Philadelphia (*Barry Lyndon, Sunshine Boys*), night-club acts that opened when I was out of town (Alaina Reed at the Grand Finale, Martha Reeves at Reno Sweeney). Leafing through magazines—stacks of *Hollywood Reporter, New York, Time, Michael's Thing*. Tearing up casting announcements, press releases, notices of publishing-day parties—stuff that would take another month to catch up with. All in the waste-paper basket. I have the Knight story to write as priority, but first I must scare up a couple of columns.

Shirley MacLaine, whom I've written about before, is a good choice. Shirley is taping a TV show called *Gypsy in My Soul,* and her press agent has invited me to watch.

Lucille Ball, he says, is Shirley's guest. Maybe I can get two columns out of it.

As it turns out, both star ladies are cooperative. I don't have to speak much to Shirley—the thrust of the column is the madness that goes into a TV taping. One of the show's dancers is somebody I had a brief fling with a year before, and during a meal break, he tells me that when he first came to New York, he'd stand for hours in front of Shirley's apartment building, waiting for just a glimpse of his idol. "And now look at me. I'm dancing with her." It makes good copy.

Lucy Ball is another matter. She invites me to her dressing room, and talks as if I were her oldest friend. I don't think it matters who I am. She just feels like talking.

She isn't hard-nosed, callous, tough, but she is vulgar as well as gracious. She offers a bourbon. It's a miniature bottle that she took from the plane that flew her to New York. Three more of them are in her purse.

Between swigs, she discusses Jack Benny's death, *Wildcat*, and a 1939 film titled *Five Came Back*, which has just been shown on television. Then Lucy tells a remarkable story about what it's like to be a mother in a world of changing moral values.

It seems that Lucy used to screen movies for her family at her home in Beverly Hills and when the children were growing up, she had a rough time finding the right films for them. She showed *Thunderball*, which seemed okay until Sean Connery as James Bond crawled into bed to make love to a naked woman. "Stop the movie, stop the movie," cried Lucy, and the projectionist stopped the camera. After that, Lucy decided that she had to be more careful about what she showed. She had her secretary cautiously check through the lists of each distributor. Clint Eastwood cowboy films were acceptable, but there was little else and the kids were getting bored with cowboy movies. So one day, Lucy ordered a *National Geographic* catalogue. She liked the titles they listed. She thought, What could be more perfect than a nature film with a stirring narrative about the aurora borealis or a documentary on the plight of the American buffalo? So she showed a few travelogues. Her kids liked them, too. They were educational and interesting.

Then, one day Lucy heard that a film was made called *The Fox*. That should be nice for the kids, thought Lucy. She instructed her secretary to get a print. So there they were, the entire family in the comfy of the living room, watching a movie that opened with a beautiful scenic shot. "Just like an Andrew Wyeth painting," said Lucy to her family. And then there was that sweet Sandy Dennis milking a cow. And that other woman churning the butter. Lucy wondered why that other woman was churning the butter with such passion, wearing that plaid shirt and jeans and men's boots. And suddenly, she knew. "Stop the movie, stop the movie," yelled Lucy. The family never got beyond two reels of *The Fox*.

I laugh loudly at Lucy's tale, yet am bothered by it. On my way home from the interview, I realize why. I'm reminded of another tale told to me by New York city councilman Carter Burden. Like Lucy, Carter had spent part of his life in the palatial manors of Beverly Hills. His father was a financier and his mother a niece of Douglas Fairbanks. Both parents were liberal and open-minded. "They wanted me to know all about life," said Burden. "And I'm glad they did. Fear of exposing youngsters to life-styles that are considered 'different' is perverse. Children should be exposed to the world in their formative years when they have good sense and judgment.

"In California, I saw adults suffer from the kind of

spoken and unspoken prejudice against homosexuals that is still prevalent in this country. These people learned to hate themselves. They disguised themselves, they tried to 'pass.' They'd have been happier and healthier if they were able to express their feelings and live openly.''

Burden admitted that the genesis of his sponsoring the gay civil rights bill in New York came from that climate of closet he'd witnessed in the posh parlors of his youth.

The theme repeats itself. Homosexuality is bad. If you are gay, you are not an acceptable person. So you hide your gayness. You make fun of the people who are obvious. You try to pass for straight. You get to hate yourself. It's the theme of many lives—the reason for the gay liberation movement—the theme of John Knight's life. And the theme of the *Voice* article about him.

The piece is tough to write. I bundle up and lock myself in my cold apartment for over a week. A friend comes in to cook. The answering service takes calls. The only calls I return are those from Tom Morgan, the *Voice's* executive editor.

I know there'll be flak on the story. Whenever I crank out a gay-oriented piece, the walls come tumbling down. No matter how sensitive the writing, any article that deals with a gay-style murder is bound to incite half the homosexual population. Some yell, ''Why hide a killing? You have to warn our people. Don't suppress the news.'' Others shout, ''Why do you have to show our moles and not the good constructive lives we lead? You're giving the homophobes fodder to proliferate their hatred.''

Maybe so, but cultivating petunias in a window box

with a lover in King of Prussia is not news. It's not interesting to me—doing it or writing about it.

When I put the last period to the story, I'm not entirely happy with its structure. It takes too long to get started. Fortunately, Tom Morgan assigns the best editor we have at the paper, Karen Durbin, to iron out the kinks. Karen and I go over the article, line by line. The *Voice* lawyer vets it. And it's ready to run.

At the paper, there's a lot of excitement about the piece. Clay Felker says he thinks it's terrific. Still, I'm afraid that because of its length and specialized theme, the story will be hidden in the back pages. Movie critic Molly Haskell has written a first-rate feature on filmmaker Lina Wertmueller which seems the likely cover story. But the powers that be finally opt to run with the Knight piece on the front. They title it "The Fatal Consequences of the Secret Life," a title I'm not mad about since many secret lives don't have fatal consequences. A photo of Salvatore Soli runs on the cover. The shot was taken right after his capture in Miami and shows him wearing a shirt with a raindrop and polkadot pattern. An inside shot shows John Knight wearing the same shirt. One can conclude either that the shirt was ripped off from Knight by Soli, or that raindrops and polka dots are popular in Philly.

When the paper hits the stands, the reaction is mostly favorable. There's a fan letter from Lacey Fosburgh, who writes for the *New York Times* in San Francisco, and who has just completed a book on the *Looking for Mr. Goodbar* murder case. Lacey claims that she's taken out a subscription to the *Voice* as a result of the Knight piece.

Among the negative responses is a letter from a young Bostonian who writes that I'm too nice to the Philadelphia police on their interrogation of gay people.

The loudest cry is from the Aesthetic Realists, a philosophical group founded by Eli Siegel. One of their missions in life is to cure homosexuals. "The newspapers can prevent the perpetuation of the cycle of violence, sensationalism, exploitation, and guilt associated with homosexuality and the milieu that surrounds it by printing news of Aesthetic Realism," writes an intrepid Realist. He signs his letter "Victim of the Press."

From Philadelphia, my florist friend phones to report that he's heard from all of his Christmas dinner guests and they were delighted to have met the author of the article. "What do you do for an encore?" asks the florist.

I tell him I'll be back to cover the trial and ask that he keep me posted on Knight-related events in the interim. His hurt voice suggests that we see each other long before the trial begins. I invite him for a weekend of fun in New York. He accepts. It isn't fun.

In the months that follow, newspapers report a couple of cases that bear similarities but are unrelated to the Knight killing. Actor Sal Mineo, coming home from a rehearsal of *P.S., Your Cat Is Dead*, is ambushed in an alleyway outside the garage area of the apartment complex where he lived near Hollywood's Sunset Strip. Neighbors heard him scream, "My God, my God, help me!" They saw a man wearing dark clothing running frantically from the scene. Mineo's body was discovered moments later, blood seeping through his blue jeans and windbreaker. He had been knifed in the chest and side and there had been no sign of robbery.

(Nearly two years later, a Michigan convict allegedly bragged to fellow inmates that he stabbed Mineo in a robbery attempt. The convict was extradited to Los Angeles and booked on a murder charge.)

A week or two after Mineo's death, *Newsweek*

printed that "whispered reports on the actor's alleged bisexuality and fondness for sado-masochistic ritual quickly surrounded his murder; one acquaintance went so far as to speculate at the murder scene that 'it was a new boyfriend or something. They do have their quarrels.' " In the same article, director Peter Bogdanovich noted that the thirty-seven-year-old Mineo had "strange tastes."

Having met Mineo, and having seen him at several New York parties, I'd say his tastes ran toward very young, angelic-looking men who posed and sulked and wore leather jackets.

Two months after Sal Mineo's death, internationally known decorator Michael Greer is found strangled in his Park Avenue apartment. There's evidence of at least one powerful blow to the head, and a strange liquid flowed from Greer's mouth "like someone had poured blue paint on his face and it had dried," claims the woman who discovered his body. The woman recalls that Greer was clad only in a blue kimono, lying face up in bed with ankles bound together by a black-and-red ascot. For some odd reason, framed photographs, including one of actress Bette Davis, are turned face down in the room where he died.

Greer, an acknowledged homosexual, had fallen into bouts of depression and alcoholism and had sought out young male hustlers as his business fortunes declined. (Several weeks after his death, police arrested Greer's male secretary and charged him with his murder.)

Both the Mineo and the Greer cases are played up big in the papers. Perhaps the Knight murder led the way. Perhaps it was inevitable. Greer, in particular, is an old-fashioned-style killing where the homosexual is victim, not victor—the kind of crime that would have been played down or avoided completely in the press prior to 1970. Far different from the Littlejohn Wojtowicz bank robbery, which was made into the movie *Dog Day Afternoon*. Here, the homosexual was top man on the "macho" pole, shouting his gayness from the rooftops, demanding that his transvestite "wife" be brought to the bank in Brooklyn where he held nine hostages at gunpoint. That little incident gave the world a topsy-turvy look at the gay man who was suddenly doing it to others, as opposed to having it done to him.

Victor or victim—as the homosexual becomes more visible, media is suddenly covering all manner of happenings from lesbian motherhood to backroom bars to church-blessed weddings to murders.

In April, the Supreme Court rules that individual states can prosecute and imprison consenting adults for committing sodomy in the privacy of their own bedrooms. The decision is a blow to the cause of civil liberties, a further indication that the country has taken a swing toward the right. Congresswoman Bella Abzug tells me that "the decision is basically a reflection by the court on their unwillingness to embrace life's realities. I've always found the court self-conscious on the subject of homosexuality."

But the ruling affects all citizens on questions of privacy, such as birth control, abortion, and almost every sexual practice, save the missionary position, between husband and wife. Naturally, there is outrage among liberals. Naturally, the *Voice* asks me to write a story. During a three-day period, I speak to Ed Koch, Al Goldstein of *Screw Magazine*, executives of the American Civil Liberties Union, city councilmen, several gay liberationists, and the corner grocer. The story is heavy with quotes, light on theory, and highly forgettable. Frankly, my heart isn't in it. My head is still in the Knight case.

I decide to take a trip to Detroit to talk to some of Knight's old cronies and to visit his old hangouts. But first, I phone Billy Sage. He's living in Wall Lake, a Detroit suburb. Will he see me?

"I have my own feelings about how it was handled," stammers a voice that sounds as if it is owned by a 1966 hippie, a voice whose language is "man" and "cool" and "you know." The dialogue, however, is more "poor me" than "let the sunshine in."

"Man, they said John didn't have a will," moans Billy. "He was my best friend. If he had a will, I know he'd have left everything to me.

"John said I was going to be his partner for the rest of his life. I kept visiting him when he left Detroit for Philadelphia. It was even better then. I knew him for about five years. I knew him better than anybody. He was like a brother. Sure, we balled together, but that wasn't faggot balling. I don't think he was killed because they thought he was a faggot. He was killed for something else.

"Even John's grandfather doesn't know exactly why it happened. With all his money, he can't bring John back. I wonder how he took his murder. Probably guilty as shit. Money can't stop guilt, man. Everybody has their own little kinks. Some show them. Others hide them away. John was into hiding his kinks. He wasn't a sadist or a masochist, like they made him out in the papers. With me, he was a friend who helped out a little.

"I've been racking my mind ten hours a day over things he said to me. I guess I shouldn't have let him go to Philadelphia. When he got there, he let himself go astray again."

"Go astray? How?" I ask. "Drinking, cruising, what?"

"Everything, man. Everything. With me, he knew there was one person he could trust. He knew my father. We'd go hunting together. He knew it was cool. Sometimes he wanted more. And sometimes I wanted more. So I had to have a hard attitude about John. He never could love anybody all the way. Weird. It was meant to be.

"Shit, talking brings back the memories. I get fucked up. Memories aren't worth it. I have my own feelings to deal with.

"Look. Nobody can help John now. Not me, anyway. I can't help him. He's gone. I've got to live. I'm living and working. I do a shit job at a restaurant ten hours a day and I want to keep it, so I don't want to talk about him no more. I'm married now. I'm not a faggot. I'm cool.

"I just want to be left alone. Because I blame myself, you know. I blame myself that I wasn't in Philadelphia when that thing happened. It might not have happened.

"Since John died, I've had a hard time getting along. He used to send me money. I was going to school. Then I quit school. We talked about my going to Philadelphia to be his valet. His family didn't even want me at the funeral. I can't talk about it any more. I want to be left alone."

Detroit. The Howard Johnson's Motor Lodge near the *Detroit Free Press* building. I check in, then walk the downtown area. It resembles a dilapidated set from a long-ago production of *Dead End*. Coney Island hot-dog stands, cutrate record shops, shoeshine parlors, discount stores offering "going out of business" pocket computers at "last-time final prices," rundown movie houses playing John C. Holmes and Jennifer Welles, clothing shops with hotshot zoot-suit displays on lop-sided mannequins, and pop poster emporiums specializing in "Come to Motor City" flags and "Smile" buttons. Obviously Detroit has taken a num-ber of hard blows over the years. Decay has set in, and when it drizzles, as it does on the day of my arrival, the

stench is difficult to take, even for a New Yorker ac-
customed to peak air pollution.

To Woodward Boulevard, and a couple of gay bars.
Usual old-time eyes-in-the-mirror stuff. Impatient.
Tired. I return to Howard Johnson's before midnight,
turn on TV, and fall asleep during a Maria Ouspenskaya
scene in *Tarzan and the Amazons*.

Morning. Feeling fresh as a spray of Binaca. Walk the
two blocks to the *Free Press*. Ladd Neuman, assistant
city editor and Knight's one-time boss and friend, greets
me in his shirt sleeves in one of those bullpen offices
straight out of Kafka. He says that we'll be interrupted
wherever we talk in the building, but suggests that we
try the restaurant on the ground floor.

Neuman looks to be about thirty-three, with the kind
of face that sticks with you only after you've seen it
three or four times. Pleasant. Nonthreatening. Folksy.

He orders coffee. "I decided a long time ago," he
begins, "that I would cooperate with anybody legiti-
mate who'd want to write about John. So far, I've
written nothing myself. Someone else wrote the initial
story in the *Free Press*. It was one of those 'You really
should have known him' articles and it came out before
John's homosexual street life was revealed. Frankly, the
piece was an embarrassment."

Neuman hands me about two dozen Xerox copies of
articles with Jack Knight by-lines. Several were written
in October 1972 and involve the city court system.

"Read them," Neuman says. "They're good."

He reveals that he first met Knight in September 1970.
Neuman was chief of the *Free Press*'s local government
bureau and John had just been assigned to work for
him.

"There was a lot of competition among the Knight
papers as to who would get the kid," remembers
Neuman. "His grandfather wanted him placed some-

where where he could find out quickly whether he was any good as a reporter. They sent him to my bureau because it was a defined situation where John would have to produce quickly. Favoritism is not what they expected.

"Deliberately, they loaded the department with two other really good news reporters, both John's age. They wanted to find out if the golden boy could write as well as these other kids.

"I rode him hard. John hadn't any real experience. He had done a little intern work, but had no real writing background. I was trying to push him into shape and spent a helluva lot of time with him. His first job was to report on the courts. After that, he went through a potpourri of jobs. For a while, he was a teamster and jumped papers. Then advertising. John couldn't stand the commercial part of the business. He took off from work a lot when he was in advertising. But he did pretty well when he worked under me. He wasn't a heavy thinker. Read the clips and see."

Neuman points to an article with the headline DRUNK ARRESTS CLOG CITY COURTS AND JAIL. From what I can make out, Knight's style was along the lines of Breslin and Hamill, but not quite as terse or tough.

"John's mind was crisp," declares Neuman. "At basic reporting, he was good: a little melodramatic, but a clean writer. Police stories he did best. Anything that dealt with excitement, that kept his blood bubbling. He was a terrific lead reporter. Just the other day, we were saying we wish we still had him at the *Free Press*. Not as an editor or a soft-news guy or an analytical genius who could sit down and write a good think piece. John didn't go that way. I'm certain he would have been successful in the reporting end, even without the help of his grandfather. But Grandfather was kept abreast of his headway all along. The brass here kept him informed on how John was progressing.''

"Did the brass like him?"

"Yes and no. At the paper, John constantly talked about his prominence, about his great plans of taking over the Knight chain. When somebody would get him mad, he'd toss out a cute line like 'This is going to be *it* for you when I own this paper.' He loved the power and the money. He had a lot of money, and was spending it fast.

"But John was easy to get along with, especially when he was hosting. In a social situation, he was the perfect gentleman.''

When the clock struck six, Knight frequently ran with the rest of the reporters. They'd split for a night of cavorting, starting at a cheap bar where John often picked up the tab for everyone. Then he'd decide that this was the perfect night to do something wild, so he'd call up a limousine service and have a car take the gang to the next bar—in style.

"It was showing off," says Neuman, making little circles in the water that has spilled on the table. "No matter what the psychological reasons, John enjoyed showing off. He had a big orange boat with white fur upholstery and twin Chrysler 260's that would do about sixty miles an hour. In choppy weather, he'd rip across the Detroit River. It was suicidal, the way he raced that thing. When he tired of it, he traded it for another symbol—a Picasso. He liked to play with his money. Showing off was a major trait.

"Women? Sure. He dated a few, but no one heavily. Many of his dates worked at the paper.''

I ask Neuman for names. He mentions that one of John's dates was the paper's movie critic, another a receptionist, but cautions that I'll get nothing from them because nothing ever happened.

Did they come back the morning after and discuss John's prowess?

"No," replies Neuman. "He dated them like friends, which is to say that he'd take them out to a show, and that's it. John's women were two types: the *Detroit Free Press* kind who were safe acquaintances, and the women he didn't know and would screw around with. Those he called foxes or foxy chicks. He'd brag about how great they were. 'She had a helluva body' or 'She was good in bed.' "

Did John ever say what he did in bed? Neuman's face grows pensive, as if he's trying to reconstruct a scene that happened a million or so years ago. Finally, he lights on the scene and remarks that John was never specific as to whether his taste ran to oral or anal or self-abuse or S & M or fetishism or whatever, but there was a woman who worked in the mayor's office who once said something.

"This was a real likable girl," recalls Neuman. "She was a free-spirited woman who was nicknamed Miss Zipper because of a zipper dress she had which came off easily. When I knew her, she was making it with someone at the bureau and driving him out of his mind. She'd talk very freely about her sex life, too. Well, one day she came in and said she was 'freaked out.' I asked 'Why?' 'Well,' she said, 'I made it with John last night.' And I said, 'You did? What about your other friend?' She answered, 'Actually, John's a better fuck than my other friend.' I then asked if she was going back for more. 'No,' she said, 'because I sort of felt like one of his possessions. I got freaked out by being shown everything in his apartment, from his stereo to his etchings.'

"Because of that kind of feedback, I never suspected John had a homosexual street life. I just thought he was kind of stuck on himself. I assumed he wasn't letting women get close to him because of his money, but I remember thinking that it's still odd. Why didn't he ever have a good, heavy, long-term romance going? What the hell was he afraid of? Was he hurt in the past? Every now and then, he'd mention some girl whom he claimed he was pining for in London. That girl, he said, had gotten herself married to someone else.

"Now if you sit and talk with some of the *Free Press* reporters, they'll tell you, 'I thought maybe John was gay because he dressed too macho or because Billy Sage had called him at the office.' Shit. I knew John better than anybody in Detroit, and I didn't know his secret. In fact, the one or two times that I had any reason to suspect anything, I kicked those reasons off because John was coming on so strong with the foxy-chick rap. He'd constantly barrage me in a kind of locker-room way about the newest girl in town. I didn't know what to make of his mysterious sexual appetite. Was it real, or a cover-up for something else?

"One night, we went to what was Detroit's rowdiest, raunchiest topless go-go joint, the Golddiggers Lounge. We drank ourselves blind and closed the place. John kept trying to put the make on one of the waitresses. She wouldn't go along with it. So we finally left the bar, and John spotted this same waitress outside and took off after her. I figured he was going to get himself in trouble because you don't run up to someone in the street in Detroit at two thirty in the morning, no matter who you are.

"John talked to her like a Dutch uncle. She was really dynamite—not too bright—and the next thing I knew she was walking back to John's car. Later, I asked him how he finally managed, after having failed to entice the waitress in the bar. He said he told her he had a great record collection and a terrific stereo.

"However you sort out John's sex life, it existed

almost totally in the streets. Whether it was male or female, he'd go for that gutter level.''

There was another rinkytink bar John liked for pickups. It was called Willis's. At Willis's he met a hooker named Naomi who acted as both sex partner and pimp for him. Occasionally, Naomi would visit John's apartment with another woman. It would always be late, after the bar closed. The three would go at it till the early-morning hours. At work, the next day, Neuman would ask John, "What happened to you? You look debauched.''

John's answer? "I drank myself blind last night and phoned Naomi and she brought one of Detroit's finest to my pad. We were up all night, and we weren't reading Schopenhauer.''

Neuman looks at his watch. He waves off someone approaching the table. "They want me upstairs. I can't give you much more time," he says, "but let me backtrack. I have to, in order for you to understand our friendship.''

He explains that from the very start, John was close to him and his wife. Since Knight had no family of his own, they became his surrogate family. John would come over to their cottage for Sunday dinner and he and Ladd would get drunk, then sit out on the dock most of the night catching fish. The next day, they'd sober up and John would goof off playing with the Neuman kids. He loved children—he was godfather to their son—and would have given his right arm for a few of his own. There was always that big struggle within him.

"The struggle was that John had an idealistic view of family. He wanted a perfect wife—bright, beautiful, a showpiece—to act as hostess and take care of his heirs. Presumably, he yearned for eight or nine little Knights running around a manicured estate. He'd talk about it all the time.

"What I'm really backing up into is an explanation that John and I had a big-brother, little-brother relationship, with me always playing the big brother. He would talk candidly about his family problems: Grandpa, the family politics, that kind of crap. And about his own professional insecurity. And he'd brag about his night life. Given that context, I felt lousy, as did most people who knew him here, when we began to realize that he got himself killed out of an elaborate street life which he took extravagant measures to conceal. Why didn't John think he could tell me about the other side of his personality? Had I been so unapproachable that he felt he couldn't confide his real problems to me? John went to extremes to hide that stuff from his friends and from his grandfather and all the people inside the corporation.

"I've since thought back over some of our conversations and believe there may have been a time when John was either trying to open up the subject or tip it off. It was when he told me he had gotten himself crocked one night with an art dealer acquaintance named Eugene Schuster. I asked John, 'How crocked?' He responded, 'We cruised all over town looking for some action and would have settled for a fourteen-year-old boy.' I didn't pursue it.

"Look. John was basically homosexual. Bisexuals don't go to that extreme to hide their gay feelings. There was too much *Sturm und Drang*, too much conflict within John about his homosexuality. It was too much a closet thing with him. Had he been casual about sex, he'd conceivably have been bisexual. That wasn't what came through. What came through was someone who was tormented."

He orders another coffee. "I'm not going to get any work done this morning, so fuck it.

"Do you know about Robin?" Neuman asks.

"Vaguely," I answer. "The name's come up once or twice. Who is he?"

"Robin is a kid who's known John since the late sixties. At Harvard, John became involved in social work—you know, the delinquent-kid, big-brother sort of thing. Robin was a ward who was assigned to him, someone who had been in trouble both with his foster parents and on the street. John was there to shape him up, to rehabilitate Robin and make him acceptable to society. Several years ago, when John was interning at the *Miami Herald*, he wrote a story about a kid from a broken home who sounded very much like Robin. Except he gave the kid a different name.

"Anyway, John kept track of Robin all these years. When Robin was in Detroit, he'd call John at the paper and they'd talk on the phone for twenty or thirty minutes a throw.

"And when Robin visited Detroit, he'd stay at John's apartment for a couple of days and I'd join them for a meal or two. Robin's manner? Strictly a street person. He talked with a deep Eastern accent and sounded like a high-school dropout. By that, I mean he knew nothing about nothing. He was muscular, rough-hewed, and dressed casually, like someone who had just walked off the beach. I wouldn't have guessed him to be gay. Maybe a hustler. Robin impressed me as a hustler who knew a quick way to pick up fifty dollars. When the money wasn't coming in fast enough, he ran to John."

Early police sketches of the alleged murderers showed one of the suspects wearing a stocking cap. Robin wore a red stocking cap which was sort of his trademark. For a couple of days, Robin had been sought by Homicide detectives. They finally located him in a Florida jail cell, where he had been languishing since before the morning of December 7, so the Philadelphia police quickly ruled him out as a suspect.

Legitimately, they had reason to suspect Robin. Several months before Knight's death, he had put the squeeze on his longtime benefactor. Robin had threatened to expose Knight as a homosexual because Knight had cut him off financially.

It's difficult to know where generosity stopped and protection money began with John Knight. Obviously, kindness of heart wasn't his only motive in doling out cash to Robin and Billy Sage. Did he feel he had to take care of the boys? Or did he pay through the nose in order to keep their mouths shut?

Either way, the pattern followed: Robin, Billy Sage, Felix Melendez: John, the benevolent sugar daddy pleading, "Let me help you, let me give you money, buy you clothes, nurture your mental needs, and let's get it on." It was like a phonograph needle stuck in a warped recording of "We're in the Money."

"Billy Sage was trying to talk John into setting him up in an expensive men's clothing operation," continues Neuman. "Billy was aggressive in his monetary demands.

"No matter how you slice it, John would have eventually been exposed. He was forced to take care of several people because of his involvement in back-street affairs. Something had to give, and he probably knew that. And he grew more and more paranoiac about exposure. I'm certain he didn't want to take a chance on being cut out of the will. During the last five years, he never wavered. To be top man was his life's ambition—to run the newspaper empire, to have the power and money, to be the publisher, and to write a daily column like his grandfather once wrote."

Did Knight ever talk about his father to Ladd Neuman?

"Quite a bit," Neuman acknowledges. "John felt hurt that he was never able to know him. He had war pictures of his father displayed prominently around his Detroit apartment. The photos showed John's dad in an army uniform."

John as son. John as father. John as big brother. John as little brother. What was he? A walking role reversal? Was there no sense of self? I put it to Neuman. Did John play father to the kids he picked up?

This one throws him. "I don't know," he responds. "I'm rather skeptical. I'd guess he saw himself more in a guardian role. I'd guess he took responsibility for his tricks and wanted them dependent on him.

"Maybe you've had other people tell you this, but John wasn't a fountain of firmness."

"Yes," I reply. "I've had other people tell me this."

"Most of the time, he'd be just good fun to hang out with. By 'most of the time,' I mean when he had his head screwed on right."

With his head screwed on right, John wasn't a namedropper or a socialite in the cafe-society, picture-in-the-paper sense. His name never appeared in the columns, he rarely attended the tony social functions. A few years ago, however, he took actress Leigh Taylor-Young—once married to Ryan O'Neal—to an opening, and talked it up to his colleagues as if he were a starry-eyed housewife who had just won a trip to Hawaii on a quiz show. In his travels, he also got to know Henry and Cristina Ford. They invited him to a couple of their parties, but those particular bashes tended to be catchalls with tons of people present, as opposed to private dinners in Grosse Point. In 1972, when John gave a theater party, Henry and Cristina were among his forty or so guests. John and the Fords were on friendly terms, but they were never close.

"John liked quality," adds Neuman. "He was a connoisseur of excellent food and liquor. He appreciated good wine and drank a lot of it. When he'd drink at home, he'd go through a bottle of Schenley's scotch and, boom, empty it. Or he'd drink Smirnoff's 100 proof vodka and sail through a bottle of that.

"Drugs didn't excite him. Sure, he smoked marijuana. As far as I know, he tried coke only once. Grass was smoked maybe a couple of times a month, but then he'd haul himself out and get totally stoned. John was an excessive type. Definitely an excessive type.

"When I found out about his death, I cried a lot. I felt really rotten. At first, I couldn't tell my four-year-old daughter. She was so fond of him. She called him Uncle John. Around Christmastime, it dawned on the child that Uncle John hadn't visited as he always did. She asked me about that. I told her John had died. She cried for weeks and months after. She told me about how bad she felt about Uncle John. She tried to understand death."

Two strangers meet in Philadelphia. Both men die. And one man's death makes a child cry in Detroit.

As I leave Ladd Neuman, I think of the plot of an old movie titled *It's a Wonderful Life*. Jimmy Stewart is about to commit suicide when a kindly old angel stops him and says, "Think of the many people whose lives you've affected. Every man's life touches another's life." The deaths of Melendez and Knight have touched too many lives. They've touched mine.

Walking in the downtown debris, I suddenly have this morbid flash. Supposing I had met these two men while they were still alive? Would I have bothered with more than a polite conversation at a party or in a bar? I think so.

Would I have tried to pick up either one? I think yes. Both. For more than a one-night stand? I doubt it. I wonder. Maybe.

• • •

Not far from the *Free Press* is a block dotted with antique shops and galleries. Lester Arwin runs one of the galleries. He's in his early sixties, and his wife, who helps him at the store, is perhaps a few years younger.

The Arwins met John Knight about the same time he met Ladd Neuman. When Knight moved to Detroit, he had a painting that needed framing, which he took to the Arwins' shop. He also had a great need for new friends. The Arwins took care of both needs. John adopted the pair as his surrogate parents.

John Knight and Lester Arwin had much in common. John had been in analysis. Lester had taught a course in psychoanalysis at N.Y.U. and had been heavily analyzed. Consequently, John was freer with the Arwins than with most people.

Soon after their first meeting, John asked Lester to read a thesis he had written at Harvard about Abraham Lincoln. The paper contained some psychoanalytic information about Lincoln as a powerful man without a father. Parallels between John's search for a paternal figure and Lincoln's search appeared highly likely to Arwin. In fact, Arwin believed that John thought he had found a father in him. Arwin was about the right age. He was sophisticated, and seemed to care about John's welfare. Although Knight's quest for surrogate figures had turned into an obsession, he was nevertheless discriminating as to whom he chose. Lester Arwin was a likely choice for paternity.

"When I found out about John's death, I was just plain mad," says Arwin, taking a break from smiling at shoppers who aren't buying this particular afternoon. "I felt angrier with John because he was dead: far angrier than I ever felt when he was alive. Why? Because he had no business buying kids in the street.

"John's to blame for his own murder. Even an idiot

understands that there's no market for teen-age prostitutes without consumers. I guess John was hooked, the way a heroin addict makes a rich man out of the pusher.

"Another reason for my fury is that John didn't feel free enough to come to me about his homosexual problem. He could have told me anything, and it would not have affected our relationship."

Redundant. I've just listened to the same rap from Ladd Neuman. Could it be that if Neuman and Arwin had known, had understood, had sympathized, that their knowledge would have prevented Knight's murder?

Arwin continues. He pontificates, savoring every syllable, as if each delicious morsel from his mouth was meant to go down in history.

"I'd have guessed John liked himself too much to chance disaster. He was stuck on himself and talked himself up all the time. If he was delighted with an accomplishment, he'd dwell on his achievement until you'd never want to hear about it again. Thank God I wasn't in Philadelphia when the murder happened."

"Could you have been?" I ask.

"You bet. My wife and I could easily have been the couple at the apartment instead of the McKinnons. John had asked us to visit him. He was always asking us to spend a weekend with him in Philadelphia. It's a stroke of luck we didn't take John up on his offer. Have you seen his place? Quality. It figures. His apartment was yet another symbol of power. John was a glutton for good stuff, a hedonist. His penis was misdirected, though. Always whoring around, always ogling any girl with great tits. He gave the impression of a man about town, one who wouldn't mind going anywhere in the world for a good lay, very much the sexual being, the strong macho type, the male animal. He had me completely faked out.

"Only once did I suspect him of being gay. It was the first time he brought Billy Sage into the gallery. Sage was wearing jewelry that shook and rattled. Flashy stuff.

"John doted on him. The dynamics were interesting, so my antennas went up. John and Billy weren't in the same league. I felt something wasn't kosher, but dismissed it quickly."

After that Billy kept away from the Arwins and John seldom discussed his young friend with his older friends. Lester, however, knew that the two had gone scuba diving together and that they had lived together for a brief spell at John's apartment in the Jefferson.

"I didn't care for Billy," admits Arwin, "because I found him difficult to talk to. But I can't be any madder at Billy Sage than I can at John Knight. After all, John was shelling out the money.

"The last time I saw Billy was at John's funeral. I was one of the honorary pallbearers. Billy pulled me aside and said, 'It's not anything like they're saying. We were great friends. Now John's family has thrown me aside and I have no money.' I didn't pay too much attention to him."

I ask Arwin if he knows about John's charity work with delinquent boys. The question tickles him. He bursts into a hearty laugh, shaking all over like a sartorial version of Santa Claus. A customer turns from the impressionistic painting she's surveying and flashes a smile at him. Arwin takes control and smiles back. Lots of smiles today.

"Pardon me. Pardon me," he apologizes while catching his breath. "Charity work. My foot. I met one of those charity cases. His name was Robin. John did him no good and I told John so. Picture John taking this scruffy kid to a restaurant and spending a hundred dollars on dinner. Why, John would shower a fortune on this Robin person, who didn't have a pot to piss in.

He'd offer him champagne and a taste of caviar and the only way Robin could repeat the taste would be to hold up a bank. No, John wasn't helping him. He was helping himself. In that respect, he was totally out of line. John may have called it charity. I call it something else.

"He made a fatal error knowing the alley crowd. John thought that because he was bright, he could cope with every Angelo and Maxie when, in reality, he was a babe in the woods. That's why he was killed. He asked for it.

"His real charity work hadn't begun yet. If he lived long enough to clear himself psychoanalytically, then, through his paper, he'd have been in a position to rebuild Detroit."

Can Arwin give me a thumbnail psychoanalytical sketch of Knight?

"I really can't," he replies. "It's too dangerous. I'll tell you he was a man who undoubtedly could have contributed a great deal of good to the world. I think I was at the point of having him take some responsibility toward society, responsibility that comes with wealth and power. If you have money and a newspaper to telegraph your views, you have the vehicles to bring about constructive change. John was bright enough to want to help Detroit. But he was still at the point where he'd rather fly to Stockholm to screw around and watch dirty movies. He was pleasure-bent, but he was young. I often thought, Why the hell should I try to direct him? He has all the time in the world left.

"No. Extensive analyzing is out. Just let me say that John must have been dripping in guilt every living moment if he had to keep his homosexuality a secret from his grandfather, from his associates at the paper, from me. He called me ten days before he was murdered and said that his grandfather had sent him a million dollars. Yet with all the cash in the world, John kept unsuccessfully searching for peace in himself, using alcohol as ether to numb his brain. On the surface, he seemed content—went wherever he wanted, did whatever he wanted, flaunting his position and wealth. Why not?

"Look. It takes a long time to become what you are. What John became didn't happen overnight. He was away from home from the time he was young. First prep school, then college, England—the rich doting grandfather, everything one could want, except inward peace, which you can't inherit.

"Money? John couldn't spend the interest on what he was going to inherit. His artwork collection alone was worth an arm and a leg. He owned a Picasso, a Cézanne, a priceless set of Rouaults—the only one of its kind in existence, and he hid it under his bed.

"Have you talked to Eugene Schuster? Schuster traded him a Picasso linecut for his yacht. Schuster will give you psychoanalysis like you never heard it before."

"Psychoanalysis like you never heard before, eh?" snorts Eugene Schuster to my tape recorder between sips of a Bloody Mary at the bar in the Fisher Building. "He said that, eh?

"I'll give you psychoanalysis, but first let me tell you a story.

"John had this yacht, you know. To him the boat was a toy that served several purposes. One purpose was to help some young people whom he considered crippled. Crippled, according to John, was anybody poor, needy, down and out. His idea was to lay his hands on them, bless them like Jesus, and make them whole individuals. So he hired these boys and girls to clean up his boat. The boys looked like the girls and the girls looked like the boys. Most of them were impoverished, uneducated

Southern hillbillies. They hung out in restaurants and
bars in downtown Detroit where they could get some
dope and make a few bucks doing whatever they did.
John met them in these dives. In some form or other, he
put them to work. He was saving them. This made him
feel terrific.

"The yacht also meant status. I'll never forget the day
he invited a high-powered judge and his wife for one of
his show-off rides. We drove the yacht to the middle of
Lake St. Clair, anchored, and suddenly John produced
a gentleman's snack of the very finest hors d'oeuvres
and magnificent French champagne. Of course it was a
deliberate attempt to impress. So typical of him. And it
worked.

"But somehow, he didn't do that with me. He never
tried to dazzle me. You want to know when we met?
England, 1969. The fact that I was from Detroit and he
was going to work in Detroit gave us an immediate
bond.

"When he finally showed up in town, it turned out
that his analyst was sharing an office with my analyst.
So I started to talk to him about my shrink sessions and
the floodgates opened. John told me about his interest
in boys. I may have been the only person in town, outside of his shrink, whom he discussed his homosexual
feelings with. Our relationship was curious. We got
together a lot, I sold him some art, yet we had very little
social life together.

"Every now and then, he'd call and say, 'Let's go
out.' I'd say, 'Sure, we'll go out. Do you want me to fix
you up with somebody?' I didn't know what to fix him
up with—a little boy or a woman."

Playing Cupid, Schuster once shot a poisoned dart
and fixed John up with a big boy named Tommy.
Tommy was perky, tall, slender, your average good-
looking All-American Homosexual Buckle-down Win-

socki type. It was to be a double date: John with
Tommy, Eugene with his woman friend. The foursome
began the evening by hitting several bars. Alcohol was
consumed as if Prohibition were on its way tomorrow.
Several rounds into the night, John started to take an interest in Schuster's date. "Not for my benefit," recalls
the art dealer. "Or my date's benefit. It was for Tommy."

After a while, John pulled Tommy aside and said, "I
hope you're not offended. In spite of what you may
have heard, I'm not into the gay scene. I'm not interested in you. And I have to get back to my apartment
soon. I have a foxy chick waiting for me there."

Tommy was floored. "What's wrong with me?" he
asked Schuster. "Did I do something to piss him off?
Do I have bad breath or something?"

Schuster told Tommy that he had done nothing
wrong, that John obviously did not feel comfortable
with a nice, educated gay boy like Tommy.

A day or two later, John confronted Schuster. "Once
and for all," he ranted, "I wish you'd stop introducing
me to your faggot friends."

Schuster shrugs his shoulders. I get the feeling that
Knight may have enjoyed Schuster as a friend bcause of
his unusual persona—a mixture of jaundiced *roué* and
Jewish mother. Was Schuster the surrogate mother in
John's life?

"John was interested in a particular *idée fixe* about a
boy," he says, "and if that boy fit a particular image,
he'd run with it."

"Do you think Billy Sage was satisfying John?"

"Billy didn't believe he was gay," Schuster replies.
"He didn't understand the homosexual part of their
relationship. Billy thought that he and John were just
friends and that he was giving John something he
couldn't get anyplace else. He was right.

"Being in psychoanalysis myself, I know that nobody

can see the back of his head without a mirror or an analyst and Billy, in some ways, was the back of John's head. He was the projection of a lot of the things John felt, but found impossible to say.

"When you look at Billy now, you see a big, hulking, pudgy blond individual. Yet there must have been something there. John was in love with him. His favorite expression was 'I love the little bugger.' Now, if I were to have a boy lover, I'd have something absolutely gorgeous, say a carbon copy of Warren Beatty at the age of fourteen. Speaking of which, do you know about Robin?"

"Lately I've been hearing a lot about Robin."

"Robin is worthy of a paragraph in anything you write. During John's first two years in Detroit, he was constantly returning to Boston to get Robin out of trouble. Robin was ripping him off."

"You mean he was blackmailing John?"

"It's hard to call it blackmail when John gave voluntarily."

"Then would you call it putting on the squeeze?"

"Robin knew how to squeeze the juice from a raisin," answers Schuster, "and John would deliver whenever the squeeze was put on him. I know he took Robin scuba diving, bought him gifts, helped him when he was in trouble—which was most of the time—and spent a mint on the kid. John liked to give."

Schuster orders a refill and tells the waitress to bring a bowl of peanuts. "Hey, skip it. Don't bring them. I just remembered. I'm watching my weight."

He turns to me and complains that "All the things I like, I'm not going to eat. Vile, what pleasure does to the waistline. In 1970, I weighed 235 pounds. I lost about seventy-five pounds. 'Slim as a reed' is *in* this year.

"Like me, John had a propensity for weight."

Schuster pats his stomach. "Being short men and despising our physical selves, he and I talked a lot about dieting, exercise, getting in shape, giving up booze. But unlike me, John treated the help with respect—every single one of them. He gave them lavish tips and was interested in them as people. That Christ thing again. Or maybe he was playing Orson Welles as the young man in *Citizen Kane*. That's a better simile. Benevolent, but telling the underlings that he was *the man*.

"He was terrific with the working crowd, but John's reputation in the best circles of Detroit society was more difficult to define. The smart set figured he was someone to know for the future because one day he'd wield a great deal of power. By the same token, while he lived in Detroit he had no effective influence at the *Free Press*.

"I'll tell you a little secret. Several years ago, I had borrowed a million dollars from a local bank that was in financial difficulty. The bank called my loan, partly because of the pressure brought by the Federal Reserve. To stay alive, I had to take three of my companies into Chapter Eleven—business reorganization.

"I called John at the paper to tell him my woe. After all, he was a friend and I didn't want him to go into shell shock by reading it first in his grandfather's paper.

"John was terribly sympathetic. He arranged for me to be interviewed in the *Free Press* so I could give my side of the story. As a special favor, he got them to assign one of their best button-down-collar types to talk with me.

"A couple of days later, the article appeared on page three, along with a photo. Both the story and photo were disaster. They made me out the 'playboy spender,' with the 'candy-apple Rolls' and the 'lavish house,' squandering money with millions of debts. The piece was pure yellow journalism. Had nothing been printed,

I'd have been better off. To this day, I wonder if John could have had it killed or if he wanted it written that way. You're a newspaperman. What do you think?''

"Ten to one, he didn't see it beforehand."

"I bet he did. I bet he had no influence in stopping the story. The irony is, he thought it was a good piece."

We both laugh.

"More? You want to know more? I'll tell you more," says Schuster. "In those days, John had a seal coat, I had a mink coat. He was pudgy. I was pudgier. He was balding. I had long scraggly hair—I wore it shoulder length. He dressed hippieish. I dressed even hippier. A lot of people thought we looked like brothers.

"His secret life? Not that secret. On one hand, he led a social, superficial life which had nothing to do with what he was feeling. On the other hand, his analyst and I knew what he was feeling and he was writing his feelings in his diaries. So he had a thinking life and a feeling life and the two were pumices, grinding against each other."

"Did he ever talk to you about his diaries?"

"Constantly. He offered to let me read them, but I refused. Sometimes it was difficult for John to go back to his apartment and write when he didn't feel like writing and I know that he didn't make daily entries. He claimed he never let his shrink read his journals. I suspect that was a mistake.

"But don't get me started on John and analysis. God, I have this feeling of utter futility about his death. I say 'Why him?' which means 'Why me?' If society can destroy someone who, because of its demands, has to lead a double life, it can destroy us all. We all do things we feel guilty about, things we hide. We can't be ourselves in fear of the community around us. John is the victim of the class he tried to curb. If society can kill him, then what happens to each of us?''

Schuster is mumbling. His voice starts to crack. I can't decide whether he's caught a severe case of self-pity or a sudden attack of the blues, or whether he's carried away by his recollections. But I believe that he actually believes what he's telling me. Quietly, I suggest that society didn't kill John Knight. Somebody stuck a knife into him, five times.

"Society killed him," snaps Schuster. He calls the waitress and orders a third drink and tells her to bring a couple of bowls of nuts this time. Then he relates a final John Knight story.

The story begins on a night when Schuster and his pal had gorged themselves with rich food and had taken to cruising around town. It was a typical dull Tuesday in Detroit. Nothing was happening at the straight bars, so the team hit a transvestite joint packed with truck-driver types and girlies trying to outdo each other in the Brigitte Bardot look-alike department. Boredom personified.

"Let's get out of here," said Knight to Schuster after two drinks and several "get you, Mary" looks from the locals. "Are there any really great gay bars in town to see?"

Schuster thought Knight was playing Margaret O'Brien in *Little Women*, but nevertheless suggested the Wonder Bar, where they had one drink. No action there, either. They proceeded to the Town Pump.

At the Pump bar sat a kid, maybe seventeen or eighteen, with a pencil-thin moustache and Jergens Lotion skin, wearing a white flannel double-breasted jacket. Beside him sat a much older man. The older man was pawing the kid.

"Take a look," said John to Eugene. "I like him," pointing to the kid.

"I'll pick him up for you," said Schuster, figuring

there was no difference between picking up a boy and picking up a girl.

Schuster walked up to the bar. He started a conversation with the kid, his back turned toward the old man, who wasn't crazy about the sudden invasion of his terrain. Knight stood a few feet away, but within listening distance.

"My friend and I have got a red Rolls waiting outside to take you away from all this," Schuster said to the kid.

The kid's eyes all but popped out of their sockets. "A red Rolls-Royce? I don't believe you."

"Don't believe me," said Schuster haughtily. Then, from his pocket, he pulled a one-hundred-dollar bill and tore it in half. One half went into his pants pocket, the other half into the kid's hand.

"Want the whole bill? Meet us in the car outside."

The older man looked on aghast as Schuster and Knight left the bar. Once outside, Knight said, "I'm not going to do anything with him, Eugene. I'm just going to show him my scuba diving equipment."

"Sure," said Schuster. "I understand."

Three minutes later, the kid was outside, standing by the Rolls. Schuster beckoned him in. "Don't worry," he said. "We're not vice officers. We're not going to bust you."

The kid entered the Rolls. Schuster gave him the other half of the bill. They drove toward Knight's apartment building, where Schuster dropped off his two passengers.

The next day, he phoned John and asked, "What happened?"

"We talked late into the night. Nothing happened," said Knight.

The money was thrown to the wind.

• • •

In death, the camouflage eroded. Underneath the subterfuge existed a frightened, tortured boy-man. Remove one veil, then another, then another, until you find there are more than seven.

Night falls in Detroit. Eugene Schuster drives me to the apartment where John Knight lived. The building isn't as attractive or swank as the Dorchester. It's more like an expensive housing project structure, similar to the one my Aunt Julia lived in on Myrtle Avenue in Brooklyn in the early fifties. Across the hallway from Knight's old apartment, I ring the doorbell of his neighbor. The young man who appears makes me swear I won't use his name in print. He shows me around his pad, claiming Knight's place was similar in layout, if not decor. He attests to the fact that John was a wonderful neighbor, a regular loving guy. No, he didn't borrow eggs or sugar or girl friends or boy friends, but he was wealthy as Croesus and generous too and often brought him gifts. The neighbor shows me one of the gifts, a stunning piece of handcrafted pottery.

"Do you know how much it's worth?"

"No idea," I say.

"Plenty, but I wouldn't sell it. John was my friend."

Downstairs, the doorman calls a taxi. I ask the driver if he knows a spot called the Town Pump. He drives me to a bar that's housed in a hotel not far from my Howard Johnson's heaven. Apparently, the place doesn't jump until midnight. It's only 11 P.M. I take a table next to two young men, and eavesdrop.

"It's the most expensive restaurant in Detroit. You walk right in, any night of the week at nine, and it's filled with diners," chirps the brunet half of the conversation. His hair is parted on the side, longish in front, a few strands fringing the forehead. He's dressed in a print shirt with a scene depicting a tennis player holding a racquet, beige gabardine trousers, crew-neck sweater tied in a loose knot around his shoulders, high-heeled shoes that look like ice skates.

"Is it like the Pavillon in New York?" chimes his listener, a vision in a white Lacoste shirt with alligator snipping the left nipple, pressed blue jeans, white socks, and Weejuns. His canary-blond hair is permed in an Afro.

"The Pavillon? That's closed."

"Oh, yes? We used to go there all the time, for five years."

"No, that's closed a long time."

The brunet checks his digital watch. "Dull, dull, dull," he yawns. He glances at me staring and listening and loudly proclaims, "As far as I'm concerned, Uncle Charlie's South in New York is one of the greatest places I've ever been to. I love it, especially Sunday afternoons. What amazes me is that so many beautiful people fit under one roof and everyone is so friendly."

"California has better-looking men than New York," suggests the Lacoste shirt. "San Francisco has phenomenal men and dogshit women. The only men I ever met in New York were dogshit."

Masochism prevails. I smile at Lacoste and say, "I'm from New York."

"Oh, really? What are you doing in Detroit?"

I tell them both. They're half listening. They find the subject distasteful, as if someone has dumped mustard on their ice-cream conversation, but they're too polite to say "Change the record." Instead, Lacoste inquires, "So what are you doing at the Town Pump?" His eyes bat, the little flirt.

"John Knight used to come here. I want to get a feeling of his life."

"Weird. Was he cute?" asks the brunet.

"Adorable."

"But he's dead?"

"He's dead."

They don't say another word to me. Their conversation continues.

"The thing to remember," says the brunet, "is that on a push-botton phone, you get more wrong numbers."

"In Chicago, pay phones are all push-button," informs Lacoste. "Back in San Francisco, I had problems dialing. I used to have a roommate who got collect calls from London all the time."

"Why collect?"

"He was in love with a rich lord."

I move to the bar. The place is filling up. Detroit's gay scene in 1976 is like New York in 1971, with halitosis and anemia. Keeping with the clime, I order an old-fashioned.

"What?" asks the bartender.

"Never mind. Leave out the bitters, leave out the cherry, leave out the soda. Bourbon, please. Straight up."

"What?"

"Jack Daniel's. On the rocks."

There's a sudden commotion around the pool table. A game is played for "consummate sex" and the two players are Stanley Kowalski and the Hunchback of Notre Dame. Quasimodo has won, which means that he can tamper with the body of his opponent. Onlookers offer rowdy comments. A double-or-nothing rematch is suggested. "Not on your life," says the Hunchback.

I turn my attention to the pert number who's bouncing on the next barstool. "Hi. What's that music they're playing?"

"It's the sound track for *2001*," he answers. "It's old." The kid's buns stop bumping when the record stops and he fills me in on who's who at the bar. He points out the manager, standing under a red light near the exit sign. He waves at a hunk who he says is the best go-go dancer in town. He tells me that he's good, too, and asks me to buy him a gin and tonic. I do. Silently, he toys with the swivel stick. Slowly, he sips the liquid. And coquettishly, he puts his hand on my crotch. Length doesn't matter. Arousal doesn't matter. Why I'm here doesn't matter. What I'm worth does. He offers to leave with me for fifty dollars.

"You're very nice," I say, "but I don't think so."

He takes his drink and moves to the jukebox, with not so much as a Goodbye, Mr. Chips.

That night, I have a dream. A school of whales is visiting a leather bar where whales and humans mix and mingle, and are friendly to each other. The bar is on a beach and the whales also play in the water near the shore, communicating with the humans, who are wading in the shallow part of the water. The whales are not dangerous, but they are all over the place.

One whale, however, is isolated on a wall a short distance away from the others. If kept out of the water too long, this whale will die. He is reddish and sick. The mammal starts to crawl past the people on the beach, past the leather bar, back to its rightful place in the water where it can survive.

I wake up in a sweat. I don't know whether the whale makes it, whether he lives or dies. I think he dies.

Back in New York. Audrey Hepburn, Lee Grant, Tom Burke, Ted Hook, Louise Lasser: time is told by the columns that fall from my Olivetti. March is William Atherton, an "out-of-the-closet Aesthetic Realist." April is the Phoenix location story of *A Star Is Born* with Streisand bossy, Kristofferson drunk, and Jon Peters running around in white gym shorts, telling me, "My old lady's got balls." May is luncheon at the Russian Tea Room with Edie Bouvier Beale, Lillian Gish and Anita Loos ("The camera can't hide quality or spirit," said Miss Gish). May is also an event which I don't write about, a discussion on hustlers at the West Side Discussion Group.

The guest star is a male madam who is abrasive and impersonal. He wears short shorts showing great legs and a skin-tight shirt which emphasizes stomach flab. I knew the madam when he was simply one of the boys back in the early days of the gay liberation movement. Then, he was the bookkeeper for the Gay Activists Alliance. Liberation can take many pathways.

The people who pay their two dollars for the hustler-model forum are mostly middle-aged men who live in New Jersey or the boroughs with their mothers or lovers. As a group, they are warmhearted, well-meaning, middle-income, TV-viewing, cake-baking, popcorn-eating conservatives who come to these meetings to acquire culture and titillation.

Culture is not on the agenda tonight.

Our madam begins his recital by solemnly stating that his service offers primarily convenience. For forty dollars, he provides a dirt-cheap trip to paradise. His models do not dabble in blackmail. They do not engage in the old Murphy game. They are test-tried and screened—he doesn't say how—before they are sent into the field. And they receive twenty-seven dollars on the forty they bring in. Of course, the customer is expected to pay cab fare, and a tip is nice if the client is satisfied.

The business is competitive, for both model and madam. Several services exist in town, and everyone and his brother wants to be a callboy.

One can phone the service twenty-four hours a day. Many callers are screwballs. "They don't give a damn about courtesy when they're in a hurry to get it on,'' sighs the madam. ''Some screwballs request catalogs. They want to select, like they're shopping at Barney's Men's Clothing Store. And they won't settle for less.''

The madam perches himself on a table and asks if there are any questions from the audience. Some paying guests feel cheated: they had been assured that one of the madam's boys would act as co-host, but the promised model had been arrested in a hotel-room raid just a few days before and is naturally keeping a low profile. Plus, the madam's remarks aren't that provocative or scintillating.

''You really hate what you're doing,'' yells a West Sider.

''Sometimes, yes,'' answers the madam. ''Especially when it comes to the john who wants to bargain. I don't like to haggle and I don't want to operate a fruit market. If the quart of milk is more expensive down the street, you don't buy it there.''

''Do you have your models undergo periodical physicals for V.D.?''

''Sure,'' replies the madam.

''What are the standards of the models' dress?''

''The appropriate fashion to get into a better apartment building or hotel is short hair, a neat jeans suit, and a beat-up copy of the *Village Voice*.''

With the last remark, Madam glares at me. The crack elicits titters from the congregation. The questions get better.

''Does a model lose his enthusiasm?'' ''Do you report your earnings to the Internal Revenue Service?'' ''Do you go to bed with your boys?'' ''Do you charge more for specialty acts?''

Suddenly, the audience is enjoying their own daring. They can't wait to outdo each other with devastating questions, and the men posing the questions are a revelation. Undoubtedly many in the room have already used the service and many new recruits will be enlisted as a result of my old acquaintance's personal appearance.

It's better than placing an ad in the *Advocate*.

THE
TRIAL

PHILADELPHIA. MAY 10, 1976. The trial begins.

In a courtroom packed with prospective jurors, Nino Tinari, who is representing Salvatore Soli, reads a statement claiming his client is not guilty of robbery, simple assault, aggravated assault, burglary, criminal conspiracy, involuntary manslaughter, and voluntary manslaughter. All charges stem from the John Knight murder. The Felix Melendez case is to be heard in Camden, New Jersey, at a future date.

Judge Williams suggests that those who have read or heard about the case make their presence known by standing. Approximately three quarters of the one hundred people in the room rise. The judge instructs them to sit and says, "You need not give your names."

District attorney Emmett Fitzpatrick informs the panel that most witnesses at the trial will be law officials but that the jury may also hear testimony from Linda Mary Wells and Donna DePaul, who were arrested with

Soli, and Joseph Paolucci, whose house Felix Melendez lived in.

Soli's lawyer does not disclose the names of possible witnesses for the defense. He asks the potential jurors to answer questions with honesty and sincerity.

Soli's father and three of his five sisters are in the courtroom. They listen gloomily. As for Soli, he sits solemnly next to his lawyer and looks as if he is tranquilized, as he well may be. From all appearances, this is a dignified, sedate group we have here. From all appearances . . .

I check into the Warwick, call the florist, and announce I'm back in Philadelphia for the trial. He says he's glad, but he can't see me. Ten minutes later, he phones, says he's sorry, and tells me to come over. An hour later, we're on a queen-sized bed in a mirrored room with a palm tree in the corner. We ball. I've never cared for him well enough to allow inhibitions to get in the way. Tonight, it's homecoming night, so we experiment. His sexual tastes are more bizarre than mine. Baby oil, see-through underwear, mirrors, poppers, and several side trips for him to the kitchen cupboard for gulps of Southern Comfort straight from the bottle. Hardly any dialogue. Hardly any sleep. What am I to do? Stop seeing him altogether? This arrangement can't continue. I'm here to work.

With an hour's sleep and bags down to my toenails, I schlep to the City Hall Building for the first day of jury selection. Slung over my shoulder is a Danish schoolboy tote bag with reporter's notebooks, address book, pencils, cassette recorder, aspirin, cashew nuts, Lilli Palmer's autobiography, and press credentials. I stop at Horn and Hardart's for coffee and a corn muffin. Outside City Hall stands an Amazon woman with banner proclaiming "Impeach Mayor Rizzo." Several souls dedicated to saving Philadelphia approach me and request that I sign a petition. I tell them I'm not a registered voter. It's suggested that I can sign the paper anyway. I'm too bedraggled to tell them to fuck off.

Inside the courtroom, a half dozen newspaper and radio people are allotted the choice jury-box space: ours only during selection proceedings. From this vantage point, we can spot dimples and moles and even smell the breath of the women and men questioned by Fitzpatrick and Tinari. With me are Jill Porter of the *Philadelphia News*, Marilyn Schaeffer of the *Bulletin*, Vivian Aleica of UPI, Tia O'Brien of WCAU radio, and Larry Reibstein of the Cherry Hill, New Jersey, *Courier-Post*. We are destined to be comrades in the days to come. As far as I can make out, there are no representatives of the gay press in the courtroom. Not surprising. The gay papers usually can't afford to pay reporters. They tend to rewrite stories which appear in the straight media.

Soli and his attorney strut in, like two roosters, and it's a fashion show. Soli wears an emerald-green three-piece suit with light-green shirt, dark-green shoes, and avocado-green tie. The color coordination makes him resemble an Italian leprechaun—he could have stepped out of a Naples production of *Finian's Rainbow*. Soli's naturally dark hair has weathered the blond dye job nicely. He's back to being a brunet, puffed and fluffed. I'm aware of his ballsy attractiveness. He is, too.

He sits in a chair directly facing the witness stand and picks at his teeth like Clark Gable in *San Francisco*. His attention varies as each potential juror is called into the room. Undivided attention is paid to the prettier women.

Selection procedure is on an individual basis, questioning one juror at a time, in an area that's set apart from the other jurors. District attorney Fitzpatrick asks each candidate if he or she would consider the death sentence. The first juror to be chosen claims she doesn't believe in capital punishment.

"Would you consider it?"

"Yes."

She is a black middle-aged married woman with three children, employed by the Board of Education.

Juror no. 2 is young, a secretary who works for the school board, too.

More than thirty citizens are called before juror no. 3 is chosen. Tinari asks each to pinpoint the area where he grew up as well as the area in which he now lives. Strategy is to select jurors who come from lower-middle-class or poor sections. Presumably they will relate to Soli's plight, they will be sympathetic. Several are asked by Tinari to recite the titles of recent books they've read. What television shows they watch. If they listen to the news.

A college student who attended Catholic parochial schools is dismissed. A hotel clerk who lives with his family is asked whether he's married, and is disqualified, I assume because there might be a question about his heterosexuality. Most of those questioned enter the courtroom as if they've come for a do-or-die interview. They are shy and passive and nervous. None are defiant.

"I can't even think," says a woman with hair that's been cut by manicure scissors. She starts to cry. Tinari gets her a Dixie cup of water. She sobs, "I'm sorry." She's excused.

A respectable housewife carrying a copy of *Good Housekeeping* states, "I've forgotten everything I've read about the case. I can be a good juror. I always think everything out clearly." She's accepted by D.A. Fitzpatrick, but challenged by Tinari. Excused.

On it goes. Tinari dismisses anyone who might be over fifty, anyone who objects to the use of drugs, anyone who has the slightest tinge of lavender in his makeup. He's after street types. Fitzpatrick is after establishment. Tinari strikes me as oily, Fitzpatrick as slick. Both come to this case with reputations. Tinari has recently been acquitted on charges of perjury, witness tampering, and obstructing justice in connection with a municipal corruption probe in Philadelphia. Past clients include murderers and Mafia figures. He has also defended Soli several times before. He and Soli have known each other at least fifteen years.

Emmett Fitzpatrick was one of Philadelphia's top defense lawyers before being elected district attorney. His candidacy was not supported by Mayor Rizzo. Since his election, however, he has represented the Commonwealth in court only on major cases, or where it has been politically feasible for him to do so.

It is clear that Tinari and Fitzpatrick have no respect for each other. Their hostility is both entertaining and destructive. They are clearly extensions of their clients in this murder trial.

A department-store manager tells Tinari, "I followed the case pretty closely and found it interesting and made a decision about who was guilty at the time. After the publicity died down, I frankly forgot about the case. Then this morning, it all came back again. I assumed Soli was guilty. When you sit back and read a newspaper, you can form an opinion very quickly. What I have to do here is judge on the facts if I'm selected. I came into this courtroom with the responsibility of being a juror, but the impact doesn't actually hit until you're put in a position to judge a person's life."

"Can you follow the law?" asks Tinari.

"I think I can. If I hear both sides of the story, I'll be able to make an honest judgment."

Tinari asks if there was anything in the news reports that stays in his mind.

"I remember that Soli's neighbors didn't have nice things to say about him. But I think I can be fair to the Commonwealth and the defendant."

Tinari dismisses him.

Soli's eyes follow the man out of the room. He looks at Tinari. It dawns on me that they have a silent code. I spend the next couple of days trying to confirm whether I'm right about the code. By pulling at his right earlobe, does Soli signal "Acceptable"?

The afternoon drags on and there's little progress. I'm beginning to remember that I had no sleep the night before, and that I'm no longer twenty-one. As I fight to keep my eyes open, Tinari asks a candidate if she's Mrs. or Miss.

"Ms.," she announces.

The woman is black, young, and sharp. Her hair is short-cropped, she wears big hoop earrings, carries a trench coat and an air of self-possession. She tells Tinari that she works as a keypunch operator.

Soli's eyes are glued to her. Not once does she look at him. He pulls at his ear. Tinari says she's acceptable. No fight from Fitzpatrick. She's sworn in as juror no. 5. The court is adjourned until tomorrow.

Jill Porter has been covering the Knight case almost from the beginning. She's a general assignment reporter for the *Philadelphia News*, where Knight worked. In the reporters' room at City Hall, Jill tells me that she knew Knight "only in passing."

Impressions? "As a woman, when you meet a new man, you try to get a reaction from him. I got nothing. No vibrations at all. I just assumed John had other interests.

"I didn't know for weeks that he was the boss's grandson. He dressed well, and was clean-cut. There was never any indication of anything but a super-straight life. He struck me as square.

"After his death, there was a great deal of reflection in the newsroom about our profession. We were faced with an issue. Do we run or don't we run with John's 'other life'? We argued back and forth about what was immaterial and what wasn't—that question of violation of privacy. The decision was to use anything that was relative to the murder. However, I, for one, was enraged that the media took his homosexuality and distorted it way out of proportion. The dailies made him seem like the embodiment of evil. They reduced Knight to one part of his being.

"I guess the *News* didn't play up John's gayness any less than the other Philadelphia papers. The *Bulletin* was the first to allude to it. They ran the story in a late edition, then pulled it. Then we ran it, then they put it back.

"Initially, there was a fear that the cops were manufacturing the gay part. All that juicy stuff could have made us look foolish if it wasn't true. And we were skeptical not only because of the straight impression John gave, but also because the Police Department is alleged to be an arm of Mayor Rizzo. Rizzo hates the *Inquirer* and *News*."

Two months before the Soli trial, Rizzo had filed a six-million-dollar libel suit against the *Inquirer*, its three top executives, and a reporter named Desmond Ryan, who had written a satirical story in the paper's March 14 issue under the caption "Our Mayor Speaks." The article, purportedly written by the mayor, poked fun at his Honor's attitudes about institutions, his prejudices, and his colorful jargon. Five days after it was published, the *Inquirer* and *News* offices were picketed by members of the Building and Construction Trades Council.

The picket line was led by an old Rizzo ally and the picket signs read, "When is the *Inquirer* going to start telling the truth?"

Rizzo's ongoing feud with the Knight-Ridder forces raises a query as to whether John Knight's diaries will be entered as evidence in the trial. Certainly, it would benefit the Mayor to embarrass the brass at the newspaper chain just as they continuously embarrass him and certainly John's true confessions, even in death, would embarrass. Already, there have been leaks on diary content. A *News* court reporter named Joe O'Dowd informs me that he's been read diary entries by someone in the Police Department.

For D.A. Fitzpatrick to haul the diaries into court, he'd have to be damn certain they'd benefit the prosecution—and they'd have to be relevant evidence. It's possible that the jurors would be more inclined to convict Soli if they had Knight's journals in their hands. But it's also possible that the defense would be in a position to turn around and use entries to their advantage.

The way Pennsylvania law works, if you are involved in a felony murder you are guilty of murder. Doesn't matter whether you yourself pull the trigger or plunge the knife: if your accomplice has a weapon and actually commits the crime, then you are as guilty as he.

Indications are that Soli didn't plunge the knife, that he was along for the ride. But the bet around the reporters' room at City Hall is that Salvatore Soli will get manslaughter, and the Knight diaries will be dragged into court.

Second day of jury selection. Soli is in an open-collared navy blue shirt with French cuffs and cream-colored jacket featuring Joan Crawford shoulder pads. His hair is a little less teased than yesterday. His father,

Sal, Sr.; his sister, Mary; his only brother, Anthony, sit three rows in back of the witness stand. From time to time, Mary Soli throws reassuring smiles at him.

Sal is more confident than yesterday—a half smile fixed to his face as he scrutinizes each person in the courtroom. Today, his fist is clasped to his chin. Perhaps a new signal to worry about.

Key issue in jury selection continues to be the death penalty. If a person called to the stand claims he is incapable of administering the sentence, he is dismissed or challenged by Fitzpatrick. In two hours, Tinari and Fitzpatrick trundle through twenty constituents before selecting juror no. 6.

A break is called. The artist for the *Philadelphia Inquirer*, who has previously been told not to sketch during jury selection, places himself in front of Soli and starts to draw a portrait of him in charcoal. He asks Soli if he's ever wrestled or boxed. Soli smiles, but does not reply. Brother Anthony hovers over the artist's shoulder.

"Hey, that's good," he says.

I ask Anthony if he's older than Salvatore. "Ask him," he replies. Then to Sal, "This guy thinks I'm older than you."

Sal grunts.

Then I ask Anthony if their mother is okay. He mumbles that she just came home from the hospital and can't get around. He says, "That reminds me," and vanishes into the hallway to use the telephone.

In the corridor, Nino Tinari holds one of his impromptu press conferences.

"Right. You guys got it figured out. Black people challenge authority. They're what I'm looking for."

Fitzpatrick breezes by and snaps, "Don't believe a word he tells you."

Jurors 7 and 8 are chosen in quick succession. Juror

no. 7 is the first male in the lineup. One of the reporters tells me that "Save Soli" bumper stickers are flooding South Philly.

"Do you know who's got the concession?"

"No. But I bet they're not making money."

A fortyish father of four is selected as juror no. 9. Fitzpatrick asks if he's read about the case in the papers.

"I just glance through the papers. I read the captions."

"Have you drawn any conclusions about the case?"

"No. The case didn't concern me."

The woman who is to be juror no. 10 wanders to the witness stand, like Alice entering Wonderland; wavy hair cascading down her shoulders, innocent eyes. She emits a scent of wheat-germ-oil soap.

"What do you do professionally?" asks Tinari.

"I worked as a waitress."

"Where did you wait?"

"Do you want to hear all the places?"

Her lackadaisical air wins Tinari's fancy. He's avuncular with her. Soli is sold, too. He's brushing his chin and tugging his ear. Fitzpatrick steps in or, rather, tiptoes in with carpet slippers.

"His Honor will get upset if he feels you don't pay attention to him," he scolds.

"Oh, I will," she squeals.

"Can we talk about the death sentence? Do you have any fears about administering it?"

"I feel anxieties. But if any human being can possibly do that, I can do that."

"Do you feel you can be fair to Salvatore Soli?"

"I hope so."

Wistfulness, charm, and sweetness win. The young woman is accepted by both sides.

Selection continues for yet another day. Literally dozens of Philadelphians are grilled by both attorneys before jurors 11 and 12, and three alternates are firmed. Perhaps 90 percent of those interrogated are dismissed because they feel incapable of depriving another human of his life. Several of those selected for duty are as adamantly against the death penalty as many who are excused from serving, but as the hours wear on, the prosecution seems less particular about who is chosen. A couple of jurors, I feel, are selected as compromise. Yet during the entire procedure, not one individual declares that he is gung ho in favor of the death penalty. The hawks are merely doves in disguise, though sometimes it's the other way around.

Watching jury selection, one becomes aware of how basically decent most folks are. The courtroom proceeding is a sort of parade of life while the press conferences in the hallway are a travesty.

During a recess, Nino Tinari tells me that there's nothing to worry about. "The case is pure and simple. It was a fight between two girl friends who had male hormones. What happened is that Felix Melendez went in there and killed his girl friend."

I repeat his analysis to Emmett Fitzpatrick and he sneers. "Tinari could make a case against God. He'd give you eight to five against divine immortality. Sure, he has theories. But he's there to entertain you."

"Your modesty about the opposition is overwhelming."

"Well, it's based on fact."

Back in the courtroom, Judge Williams administers his opening remarks to the jurors. He tells them that they are to pay close attention to what is said. He warns that they are not to take notes: they must rely on memory. "You must be judges of credibility—I mean truthfulness and accuracy," he says. "Use your own understanding of human nature and your common sense."

He orders the seven women and five men sequestered

at a downtown hotel for the duration of the trial and instructs them that tomorrow, at 10 A.M., they are to take their oaths.

In the days ahead, the jurors are to remain a body of silent figures, each of whom has been chosen to play God in order to determine the fate of Salvatore Soli.

Late afternoon. Reporters rush to the press-room typewriters to meet early deadlines. Those who don't, phone in their stories. Everyone's busy, busy, busy. Don't know what to do with myself. Don't want to go back to the hotel. Don't feel hungry. Don't feel like writing. Don't feel like a movie. I stroll from City Hall and head back to John Knight's world. To the Dorchester. Certain entrances have been closed off. Building security is tighter. The woman at the front desk says that Knight's apartment hasn't yet been rented. They've restructured the place and broken it up into two apartments—as it was originally.

Over to Rittenhouse Square. At a pathway near the Dorchester, a kid, maybe seventeen, with fringes at the bottoms of his scarlet jeans, parades back and forth, back and forth, near a circular concrete seating arrangement. He stops. His left hand clasps his hip. He purses his lips and surveys the pedestrians in the area, like Columbus at the helm of the *Santa María*. The old Europeans with their canes and orthopedic braces and the maids and cleaning women rushing home to feed their own families are unaware that he is a gentleman of the late afternoon serving commuters for a price.

Back and forth. Back and forth. His eyes are glazy. He's stoned out of his fucking mind. Probably black beauties or Eskatrol. He flops on a bench. Up. Down. Pace. Pace. Circle.

He passes someone in leather who wears a dog collar

around his neck but who isn't a dog in the physiological sense of the word.

"Woof, Mary," he barks.

The dog collar barks back.

I leave the barkers and head toward the Dorothy Lerner shop, where Andrew Liberty works. Palm trees, bamboo chairs, and a three-foot elephant carved of oak and painted gold and red make the Walnut Street window look like the parlor of a whorehouse in Tangiers. No, Andy isn't around. "Tell him I dropped by."

To Thirteenth Street. "Dump Rizzo" tables at every second corner. Up a dark flight of stairs to the Club Baths. Identify myself. Ask the clerk if I can see the manager.

"Sorry, he's not in."

"Did you know John Knight?"

"I read about him."

"I understand he used to come here."

"Sorry, you better talk to the manager."

One of those days. Walk toward the Hasty-Tasti Deli. Place is crowded. Maybe I can pick up some info here. Take a table near the window where a fern in a ceramic hanging pot droops over my head and brushes my hair at the slightest provocation. Order apple pie and coffee. The pie doesn't have a natural ingredient in it and the coffee is rotten. Good. I can linger.

Notice that the place is very community, very fraternity. All the brothers have Vandyke beards or walrus moustaches. All wear jogging shoes and tote gym bags. None has a waistline rounder than thirty inches. Understandable. Pumping iron came in when love beads went out, and if Oscar Wilde were alive today, he'd be on a liquid protein diet.

Sitting alone in a gay restaurant, one becomes con-

scious of self and I'm conscious that I'm the only person
without facial hair, until a man, probably in his forties,
places himself at the table opposite me. He stares out
the window. His fingers tap the table, rat-a-tat-tat like
Ann Miller "Shaking the Blues Away." When the
waiter comes, he orders a ham and cheese. I suggest that
he skip the coffee. He thanks me.

Just the opening salutation is all he needs to warble
his head off. It turns out he's smart, friendly, and a
trifle vain—a fabric designer, a good one, he says
—popular and successful.

After dinner, he suggests that we repair to his apartment for a smoke. His place is within walking distance
and it's a knockout. Walls are bone-white, key pieces of
furniture outrageously bright, shining like jewels on a
sheet. He pushes a button and a panel in the bedroom
wall slides away, revealing a Sony color TV set. We sit
on the bed, smoke Colombian weed, and watch a couple
of dumb canned TV shows with the sound turned off.
Right after *Mary Hartman, Mary Hartman*, he tells me
that I'm not his type, that he likes them younger, much
younger, but that he'd like to have sex with me.

I don't tell him that he's not my type either, because I
have no type when I'm high.

We undress—separately, and without fanfare—as if
it's a ritual we've both performed a million times
before. He is aggressive in his lovemaking, demanding.
Climax is prolonged. When it finally comes, it comes
simultaneously, and I am not allowed to touch him any
more. He gets out of bed, walks to the bathroom,
showers, and returns to the room, smelling of talcum
powder. It's as if he had dropped himself in boiling
water to sterilize the wounds and applied an antiseptic.
The thought makes me miserable. I start to dress. He
says, "No. Stay." Then he tells me that he knew who I
was when we met, that he spotted me in the restaurant,

that he deliberately sat with me because he wanted to get to know me, and that he had a short-lived relationship with Felix Melendez.

I don't believe him, and tell him so.

"Don't believe me," he says. "I'll prove it."

He opens a dresser drawer and, from under a pile of shirts, produces a letter written in a scrawl that's heavy with curlicues. What it says, in effect, is, "I'm sorry. Please have me back. I love you. Felix."

I ask him if I can have the letter and he snaps, "Definitely no." He offers another joint and says, "If you're going to write about Felix, I want you to write it right." He proceeds to discuss the relationship, making himself out a martyr, and Felix a young man with problems.

When he finishes reminiscing, he asks me to spend the night with him. He tells me I must sleep at the end of the bed nearest the window and that I must sleep tight, because he's a light sleeper and wakes easily. He offers me a sleeping pill.

Poor Felix.

I refuse the pill, but stay the night.

My grandmother used to tell me that things have a way of catching up. My grandmother used to say that if you do good, you'll get good; if you do bad, you'll get bad.

My grandmother was wrong.

One hundred people push to get into courtroom no. 253. Old women, college students, welfare recipients who seek vicarious thrills by attending the "hot" trials in town. They do it because they find it exciting being on top of the news as it breaks. They do it because it's far more interesting than sitting at home watching the outcome secondhand on television or reading about the case in the papers. And many of them have nothing better to do with their days.

Some of the regulars are starfuckers: they gather outside the courtroom like autograph hounds at Sardi's and ask key witnesses to sign index cards instead of *Playbills*. Often, they'll tell a witness that they enjoyed his testimony. They comment on his clothes and his looks and speculate about his love life.

What's more, they're not afraid to express gut feelings about right and wrong, about who's lying and who's telling the truth. They seem to know what the jurors are thinking and they are positive about the outcome of each trial.

Some are knowledgeable about law, too, but impending drama is what lures them to City Hall. To miss a day in court would be tantamount to missing an episode of *As the World Turns*. The trial is a continuous saga with heroes, heroines, and villains—both among witnesses and among lawyers. Today, Emmett Fitzpatrick is the matinee idol of the courtroom set.

It's the big day, the official opening day of Salvatore Soli's trial, and Fitzpatrick instructs the jury. "The evidence really begins December 7, in a house in South Philadelphia," he begins. "Felix Melendez volunteered that he had a friend he could rip off. He got all dressed up. Then he and two other men went to the Dorchester apartments at Rittenhouse Square."

The jurors pay rapt attention as he speaks. So do Soli, his lawyer, his father, his sisters, his brother, the judge, the press, the student lawyers, the fans, the court steno, and the guards at the door.

"Inside Knight's apartment were three people: John Knight and two friends he hadn't seen in a long time. Earlier, Knight and his guests had gone out, had a social evening, returned home, and talked. John Knight suggested that his visitors go to bed after he had received a phone call. They retired to a guest room. Some time passed, when into the room came three men. Salvatore Soli was one of them.

"He made the woman guest, who was naked, look for money."

The word "naked" is stressed—uttered quick with sting, like a splash of ice water to the cheek. An effective device, perhaps, but I'm aware that Fitzpatrick is plowing it on, albeit subtly. Sophisticated theatrics work better than cheap tricks, even with the naive.

His recitation continues. He tells his spellbound audience that Mrs. McKinnon woke her husband. She gave him a weapon and ran from the apartment to get help. The elevator didn't come quickly enough. Felix Melendez entered the elevator wielding a knife. Mrs. McKinnon was cut. Her husband, meantime, rendered medical assistance to Knight. But John Knight was dead.

Many things were taken from the apartment. Credit and identification cards belonging to Knight were found in a sewer outside the house where Melendez lived. Some jewelry was found way off in Florida, where it had been pawned.

"You will hear medical evidence about the cause of John Knight's death, about his wounds and about the bleeding. I suggest you pay attention to the number and location of those wounds," Fitzpatrick instructs. Then he describes the flight. Back in South Philadelphia, he says, Salvatore Soli and Steven Maleno did not arrive at the house where it all began at the same time as Felix Melendez. Later, Melendez joined them at a motel in New Jersey. Soli and Maleno took him for a ride. Soli handed a gun to Maleno. In a deserted area near a golf course, Maleno got out of the car with Felix Melendez. He made Felix dig a hole to bury some clothing. Melendez got down on his hands and knees and while he was doing so, Maleno shot him three times and left him there. Subsequently, Soli fled the Jersey area with two women friends and ended up in Miami, where he was arrested.

The summary is brief and sparing. Fitzpatrick is interested in sketching a bare outline at first, then later filling in details. He advises the jurors to "pay attention to certain facets of the evidence: the manner in which John Knight died. You must determine the degree of homicide. Was this the intentional deed of one man or several and was it torture over a period of time or one frenzied act? We are not sure of the reason John Knight was killed from the evidence in this case. Knight was seen at one time in one place. His body moved from one room to another room. Certainly, it could not have moved by itself. What happened inside the apartment is the most important thing in this trial."

There's a break before Nino Tinari presents his opening remarks for the defense. In the hallway, the Soli ménage cluster around a woman in a wheelchair. The woman has dark bags under her eyes, gray hair pulled tight back. She appears limp, as if all hope has been drained from her life—almost a classic study in grief. She wipes her eyes with a large wrinkled hankie. Out of respect, the reporters keep away from Mrs. Soli. It is her first appearance at City Hall. Her son Anthony tells me that she demanded to be brought down. If they were going to kill her son Salvatore, she wanted to be there when they gave the verdict. She is wheeled into the courtroom and placed in a strategic and dramatic spot where she can be clearly seen by her son as well as the jurors.

Tinari begins his defense with a statement that the killing of John Knight took place after Salvatore Soli had left Knight's apartment. "The motive had nothing to do with Soli. What occurred was a spontaneous act.

Melendez and Knight were in a quarrel—yea, a lovers' quarrel.'' The reporter sitting next to me whispers, "Alas, alack. Wait until Tinari starts spouting Elizabethan couplets.''

Tinari continues. ''It all came about because of the crazed maligned mind of Melendez. These people were not normal people such as you and I. Salvatore Soli did not plan any ripoff—did not intend to do harm.''

The portrait that Tinari paints of Soli is that of a lamb who tiptoed into a panther's lair by mistake. He advises the jurors that what Fitzpatrick has related to them was not evidence. ''The evidence will come from witnesses,'' he says. ''You will have to determine whether these witnesses are credible. Whether they are biased.'' He places his hand on the banister of the jury box, and in a voice oozing sincerity, closes with, ''The events that took place December 7 will stay a long time in our memory.'' Visions of Winston Churchill dance in my head.

The court officer calls the first witness for the prosecution. He is a detective who appeared on the scene at Knight's apartment right after the murder. Fitzpatrick produces a diagram of the apartment layout, which he introduces as exhibit no. 1. Against Tinari's objections, he also enters as evidence photographs and slides of Knight's body which were taken by a police photographer. The shots are grisly: they show a dead man tied and bound like a sack of mail. The photos are passed among the jurors. Some tend to look at them for a minute or two, others offer a quick glance, and squirm in horror.

Questioned by Fitzpatrick, the homicide detective claims he found an Ace bandage in the hallway leading to the guest room. In the master bedroom, he found Knight lying on his back, his hands bound underneath him, his suit coat off his shoulders behind his back.

Knight's clothes were in disarray. His blue and white shirt appeared to have been ripped open; his chest was exposed.

As for Knight's apartment, he doesn't testify on the condition of the place, but remarks that it was specifically constructed to eliminate sound.

Tinari cross-examines the witness. He asks him to describe the paintings depicting sexual perversions which hung in Knight's gym room as well as other rooms.

"Sexual activities, not perversions," replies the detective. Tinari has no further questions. The witness is dismissed.

My gay liberationist friend Dennis Rubini, who has been sitting in the courtroom with me all morning, sidles up to District Attorney Fitzpatrick during the break. Dennis is wearing what he calls his "power outfit" instead of his customary leather. The suit and button-down collar and tie on his big frame give him an air of authority and I suspect Fitzpatrick mistakes him for an attorney.

Dennis asks the D.A. why he didn't object to Tinari's repeated use of such terms as "perverted" and "deviant." Legally, they can be considered characterizing and inadmissible.

Fitzpatrick responds that he does not want to turn the trial into a gay consciousness-raising session. "A debate over homosexuality is just what Tinari wants," he says, "and I do not intend to give it to him."

A hush falls over the courtroom as the next witness—Rosemary McKinnon—takes the stand. Patrician in appearance, stilted in posture, she gives the impression of someone who is in full bloom and the flower is a calla lily. Her manner is pristine, precise, and winning. If she blew up the Woolworth Building, she'd probably get a mild lecture from the judge.

In her lyrical British voice, the twenty-seven-year-old psychologist tells the court that she had met John Knight in England seven years ago, but hadn't seen him in two years. A week or two before his death, he phoned her husband in New Haven and invited them both to spend a weekend with him in Philadelphia.

On Saturday, December 6, she and Dr. McKinnon arrived at the Dorchester. They had dinner out with Knight and his friends, then returned to his apartment shortly after midnight, where they had drinks and listened to records for a couple of hours.

At 3 A.M., the phone rang. Knight took the call in the kitchen, returned to the den, where he and her husband had been drinking, and announced that it was time to go to bed. He suggested that they all get up relatively early on Sunday, and he'd cook an elegant breakfast.

"After the call, John was very abrupt and very strange," recalls Mrs. McKinnon, "so my husband and I retired immediately to the guest room."

Fitzpatrick asks if she ever saw Knight alive again.

She tugs at her eyeglasses. "I'm not aware of whether he was alive or dead when I saw him next.

"About four thirty, I heard voices in the apartment and a man stepped into the guest room, then stepped out again. A minute later, the lights went on, and three men entered the room."

"Do you see any of these men in this courtroom?"

Rosemary McKinnon gestures to where Salvatore Soli is sitting and says, "This gentleman over here, in blue."

Soli's mother puts her hand to her mouth and stifles a gasp. Her daughter, Mary, puts an arm around Antoinette Soli's shoulder. I hear Soli's brother Anthony mutter "Shit."

Mrs. McKinnon continues her testimony. "They asked for money and jewelry. They tried to find my husband's wallet. They searched for driver's license and credit cards and told me not to make trouble. They asked me to get up. I asked if I could get dressed. Soli wouldn't allow that, but gave me a blanket to wrap around my body. Then he motioned me to the study and asked which keys would open the desk drawers. When I replied that I didn't know, he asked if I knew where John's money was. At one point, there was a noise, and Mr. Soli pointed a gun and told me to keep quiet. I thought the noise was the security guard.

"Soli took me down the hallway to Knight's bedroom, where I saw John lying face down, in the corner of the room, bound and gagged. I heard two very deep sighs from him."

Fitzpatrick tells her to indicate on the diagram of the apartment exactly where she saw Knight lying face down. He hands her a pointer, and, without hesitation, she points to the spot.

"Soli said that they had come to settle a grudge."

"Were they irrational?" asks Fitzpatrick.

"Yes, under the circumstances, I'd say they were. They talked coherently but turned over objects and emptied drawers. During a quieter moment, Soli asked if I was freaky. He wanted to know if my husband satisfied me. He showed me some artificial penises and talked to me for about fifteen minutes, then took me to the study, where he tied my hands with a plastic bandage.

"In the hallway, they had piled up fur coats, brief-cases, shirts and other articles. Soli told me that he needed the money because he had a daughter who was ill with a blood disease and had to take care of her.

"He tied me and put me under the sofa so I was in a fetal position and placed a sofa bolster pillow in front of me to block the view. A little later, Melendez came in to look at me. Melendez spent the next hour walking back and forth between Knight's bedroom and the guest bedroom. He admitted that he was scared. He said he was all doped up and that they made him do it. He showed me his wrist with its needlepoint punctures. He said his father was a minister.

"Melendez was carrying a harpoon gun, a gun with a long barrel, and a knife."

Ceremoniously, Fitzpatrick's assistant hands him the harpoon gun and he passes it on to the court clerk. It is entered as evidence. The jurors stare at the weapon, entranced. The only sound in the courtroom comes from ballpoint pens scratching reporters' note pads.

All eyes are back on Rosemary McKinnon. "Melendez claimed he was waiting for his friends to return," she says. "No, I don't recall seeing blood on him. He asked me to come with him to Knight's bedroom. He untied my gag and cut the bandages around my wrists with a knife.

"There was a slight sound. I'm not sure what it was, but Melendez was startled. I jumped on him, took the rifle from him, ran into the guest room, and woke my husband, who had been asleep through it all. When he got out of bed, he saw Melendez in the hallway. He slammed the guest-room door shut and said, 'We must get dressed.' He told me to get help while he took care of Melendez.

"My husband now had the long-barreled rifle which I had grabbed from Melendez. But Melendez still had the spear gun and knife. He had retreated into Knight's bedroom. My husband followed him.

"Meanwhile, I tried to call the police. The phone in the den wasn't working. There was no dial tone from the kitchen phone either. I shouted to my husband that I'd try to get help outside, but didn't go into Knight's bedroom, where my husband and Melendez were scuffling.

"Instead, I ran out the apartment door, pushed the elevator button, and waited. Then Melendez appeared in the Dorchester corridor. He jumped into the elevator with me. I tried to keep his knife away, by holding on to its blade. I held him off, but cut myself on the index finger and the third finger of the right hand and also received a small wound under my left breast.

"When the elevator reached the third floor, I ran down the fire escape into the lobby and called for help."

Fitzpatrick thanks her. Tinari cross-examines. He fires a steady barrage of questions, intending to fluster Rosemary McKinnon. No way the calla lily is going to wilt.

He starts by asking if she ever wondered why John Knight was not married. Why he did not have a steady girl friend. Why he did not have a lasting relationship with any woman. "Was he as intimate with men as he was with women?" he inquires.

"Could you tell me exactly what you mean?" replies Mrs. McKinnon, icily.

"I mean were his relationships with men more than boy friend to boy friend?"

Fitzpatrick objects. Mrs. McKinnon does not answer.

Tinari proceeds to rehash the night of December 6 and the morning of December 7. He asks Rosemary McKinnon where the dinner began. What the dinner consisted of. The amount of beverages consumed during dinner. The number of glasses of wine. Of brandy. Of cordials.

"It strikes me as being a long dinner," he states sarcastically.

"Were you high, later at Knight's apartment?"

"Not particularly."

"On the verge?"

"If I was, I was unaware of it. I was rational. My husband was rational, too."

"Did your husband pass out?"

"No."

"Did you not tell the police that your husband had already passed out when you retired to the guest room?"

"I don't remember."

Tinari produces a document of the testimony which Mrs. McKinnon had given to Homicide stating that her husband had "kind of passed out." He beams as he reads the report. It is a victory for the defense. But Rosemary McKinnon remains unflappable. To Tinari's persistent pestering, she bites on her lip, clenches and unclenches her hand, but never so much as stutters. She maintains that she fell asleep on a sofa about 3 A.M. while her husband and Knight continued to drink and discuss the past. She claims that she slept for half an hour. She had looked at her watch just before dozing: it had been 3 A.M.

"Do you usually go to bed unclothed while your husband is in bed with his clothes on?"

Mrs. McKinnon doesn't answer.

Tinari's tone of voice grows progressively nastier. Having once succeeded in trapping the witness, he tries to repeat the feat, but no dice. Crisply, Mrs. McKinnon responds to his sarcasm and dismisses his innuendoes with queenly dignity. She tells him that when the phone call came from Melendez, Knight said, "That's the man who gets me girls."

"The call struck me as unusual, but I did not comment on it to my host."

"When Knight said something about getting girls, did you think he meant prostitutes?"

"Correct."

Tinari gleans from her that her first inkling of trouble came when she heard whispers behind the guest-room door.

"Were you frightened?"

"At first, no."

"Did the intruders try to revive your husband? Was he passed out?"

"He was in a very sound sleep. He had been in bed several minutes before the men entered the apartment. It was four thirty in the morning."

"When they came into the room, were they noisy?"

"There was no shouting," replies Mrs. McKinnon.

Tinari inquires if she had told anyone that Soli had taken her watch.

"No," she responds. She adds that he took off her watch while she was still in bed. "Soli stayed in my presence from 4:45 to 5:45 A.M."

It is unclear what Tinari is trying to prove. That Mrs. McKinnon lies? That she colors? That her explanation of the events of the evening is self-serving? Probably all, and more. But his attempts fail. There are no further victories. Mrs. McKinnon is like an IBM computer, spitting back data just as quickly as it's spooned in. What's more, the information never varies. More information unfolds under Tinari's prodding, but not enough to change the basic story.

She submits that she heard noises from Knight while she was tied in the living room, and that she could only assume that he was alive. "At some point, Melendez turned on the stereo. I asked him to turn it off, and he did, but he turned it on and off several times. He paced around me and kept running to the bedroom."

"Will you describe Melendez's state of mind?"

"He was frightened, upset, agitated. He said he was doped up and didn't know about drugs. The conversation with him took place in bits and pieces over a period of time. I didn't know whether it was dark or light outside."

"After you wrestled the gun from him, and gave the weapon to your husband, did you attempt to shout for help out the window?"

Mrs. McKinnon explains that her husband, on waking, opened the guest-room door. Felix was in the hallway. Felix spotted Dr. McKinnon and backed away. Her husband pursued him, while speaking to him, trying to cajole him.

"It happened so quickly—only a matter of moments. I didn't shout for help."

"When you took the gun from Melendez, did you jump on his back?"

"I don't recall exactly how I disarmed him. . . ."

As Mrs. McKinnon reevokes the experience, Tinari points to the floor plan of Knight's apartment, showing the jurors the rooms in which the various dramas occurred. Play by play, he applies his schoolmarm pointer to the chart, until Mrs. McKinnon interrupts.

"Mr. Tinari," she snaps. "You are pointing to the wrong room." Her observation demonstrates that she's paying strict attention, and it comes as comic relief. The judge smiles. Some of the jurors look as if they're trying to suppress smiles. Reporters laugh. Fitzpatrick is delighted. Even Soli manages a show of teeth.

Tinari is visibly embarrassed.

He apologizes and plows on. "Was there a conversation with the Police Department about what kind of people these people were?"

"I thought they might be gay," answers Mrs. McKinnon. "There were those artificial penises inside that plastic bag in John Knight's room, which Mr. Soli carried with him at one point."

"Is that why you believed they were gay?"

"That. And because they didn't touch me." Mrs. McKinnon removes her glasses and pinches her thumb and wedding finger together at the bridge of her nose. "And because Felix Melendez said, 'I was involved with John Knight, and he fucked me over.'"

● ● ●

The court is recessed. Rosemary McKinnon is dismissed. In the hallway, she is protected from the inquiring reporters by a scholarly-looking man whom I assume to be Dr. McKinnon. He's a foot taller, and probably one hundred pounds heavier. Together, they're a handsome couple, but on the gray side. Not their hair—their look. One of the courtroom groupies tells me she thinks "Rosemary is beautiful, and the best witness I've ever seen. But she doesn't sign autographs."

The ice jiggles in Andrew Liberty's glass. I'm on black coffee. The tape recorder is running. He's whining. He is not attractive when he whines.

Andrew Liberty is whining because he's pissed off that John Knight's mother inherited everything.

"I can't believe it. I can't believe John didn't leave a will. It doesn't figure. When there are millions of dollars at stake, you leave a will.

"John told Billy Sage that he was provided for. There was a certain Picasso that John mentioned that he wanted me to have. I've a hunch that the will was suppressed. That Billy was left a lot of things. That I was left the Picasso.

"Look, I knew John too well. He was very organized, and there were so many intimations over the year and a half of our friendship that he had everything covered. Besides which, a will would have been forced on him. For tax purposes."

The more Liberty talks, the angrier he gets. He is out of his chair now, pacing the living room of his apartment.

"Check it," he says. "The estate is still paying rent for John's Dorchester apartment months after his death."

"The apartment's empty," I volunteer.

"That doesn't surprise me. Few people can afford it. Also, it's in bad taste."

"In bad taste? I thought you decorated it."

"My decorations weren't in bad taste. The fact that he lived there and was murdered there is in bad taste. To move in would be in bad taste.

"I'm sure John had a will. He had to have a will."

I'm feeling lousy, and Liberty's juvenile display is making me feel lousier. My head is spinning. To stay longer and pass out on his Bauhaus furniture would be in bad taste. I plead tired. I am tired. Too little sleep. Too much courtroom. Knight and Melendez. Melendez and Knight. It's like searching for the lost chord, and I don't know why I'm looking. Liberty says he'll call when he's next in New York. He shows me to the door. I head back to the hotel via Spruce.

Midnight. "Come on and trade in your old dreams for new, your new dreams for old, I know where they're bought and I know where they're sold." That song. An invisible midget places a record handle at the groove in my head. "Dreams, broken in two, can be made like new on the Street of Dreams." As usual, the dreamers are out—the hunters stalking fresh quail, utilizing the crotch bulge as both bow and arrow. Sometimes it seems ludicrous—strut, express disinterest, look away, turn back to see if you're being followed, and say not a word. Ludicrous when one is on the outside, not pursuing the quail. To actively engage in the hunt, though, is a serious business. And if one lives for the hunt, and frequently misses the catch, it is a wasteful—and disturbing—business.

"Kings don't mean a thing on the street of dreams. "

I go home with one of the dreamers.

Judge Williams has just issued a gag order. He is not explaining his action. The order, he says, speaks for itself, though in this case, it really doesn't since the jury is sequestered and isolated from news reports. In effect, the order means that Tinari and Fitzpatrick can continue to hold their impromptu press conferences in the courtroom hallway, provided they talk about the sun, the moon, the stars, and true love. But they can't discuss the case.

General consensus among reporters is that the press acts as a surrogate of the public during a criminal trial, that the role of media is to gather information, and that Judge Williams may be violating both freedom of speech and freedom of the press by clamping down on Tinari and Fitzpatrick.

Both attorneys, however, are chipper as they play with the press just before Dr. John McKinnon is called to the stand. The gag order is a great vehicle for Tinari's glibness, and he rattles off weather reports in answer to reporters' queries.

By contrast, Dr. McKinnon is the soul of propriety as he is sworn in (he is, indeed, the man I saw with Rosemary McKinnon yesterday). Despite his trimness, his well-kept goatee and moustache, his wide forehead and aquiline nose, he reminds me of an afghan at a bowling alley, awkward and out of sync with his surroundings. The chair on which he sits is uncomfortable and he shifts and shuffles in it. The questions he is asked are a bother, though he condescends to answer any and all so that he can quickly return to New Haven, where he is a resident in psychiatric training. Undoubtedly, he'd offer better answers were he allowed to question himself. The answers that he gives brim with meticulous detail.

To Fitzpatrick's docile prodding, he affirms that he met John Knight in 1964 when they were both freshmen at Harvard. They roomed together at school, and got to know each other pretty well. After graduation, Mc-

Kinnon went to Cambridge to study medicine, while Knight shuffled off to Oxford to study politics, philosophy, and economics. During the following years, they continued to see each other every four or five months, though less frequently recently. Knight attended the McKinnons' wedding in 1970.

When John invited the doctor and his wife to visit Philadelphia, "I thought in my own mind that I'd pay back three hundred dollars which I owed him from college," says the doctor.

On Saturday, December 6, at about 2:30 P.M., the McKinnons appeared at Knight's doorstep. "John suggested we immediately go out. He wanted to buy flowers, and food for Sunday breakfast and he wanted to show us the neighborhood. He drove us around town and we stopped at a tavern for a glass of wine. At 6 P.M., we returned to his apartment in order to get ready for dinner with John's boss and his wife—and John's date."

Thereafter, Dr. McKinnon's testimony parallels the testimony of his wife. He states that he overheard snatches of dialogue from John's telephone talk with Felix Melendez. "That kind of conversation embarrasses Rosemary and me," he says. He also reports that much later, he woke up "to the bizarre sight of my wife standing with a rifle in her hand.

" 'Honey,' she said to me, 'you've got to wake up. Something terrible is happening. There's been a robbery. The apartment's been ransacked. John may be hurt.' She was very frightened and anxious, and talking very fast.

"In the hallway, I saw a young man, who turned out to be Felix Melendez, pointing a spear gun at my chest. I said, 'Put that down. You don't need that, you idiot.' Then I slammed the guest-room door shut and rapidly put my clothes on. I went back into the hallway, saying

reassuringly to Melendez, 'You don't need that weapon.
No one needs to get hurt around here.' He ran from me.

"I proceeded into the master bedroom, to check if
John was all right. And there, on his bed, stood Melendez, holding a spear gun and screaming, 'I didn't do it
to him.' He was shaking with fear and waving the gun.

"Apparently, he wanted to get out of the room, so I
stood away from the door to allow him to get by. Then I
chased him and caught him by the shoulders in the
hallway. I knocked him down and said, 'Stay there, you
sonofabitch.' Then I ran back into the bedroom.

"Knight was lying under a pile of debris. I knelt
beside him. His face was almost obliterated, almost
completely obscured by a number of neckties—fifteen
or more—over his nose, over his throat, in a great mask
tied tightly around his face. I ripped them all off and
saw that his eyes were closed and slightly bruised and
swollen. His mouth was open and there was blood
around it. He wasn't breathing.

"I reached for his pulse and found his hands tied
behind his back. I couldn't find his radial pulse, so
breathed a couple of deep breaths into his mouth. Then
I smashed my fist into his chest to start his heart going.
My hand was splashed with blood—there was blood all
over my fingers. I tore his shirt open and saw a massive
chest wound about two inches long. I stuck my fingers
into the chest cavity.

"Then I tried mouth-to-mouth resuscitation. I
prodded open his eyes, but knew that he was dead. It
was over. There was nothing for me to do.

"Next, I ran into the living room to call an ambulance, but the phone was dead. So I ran out of the
apartment and took the elevator to the lobby. A passerby told me that the police had just gone upstairs. I took
the elevator back to John's apartment. Cops were
everywhere. My wife was there, too. She was holding a

napkin over her fingers where she had been lacerated. I noticed that below her breast was a small knick that hadn't penetrated the chest wall.

"She wanted to go into John's bedroom but the police prevented her. To calm her, I fetched an orange juice from the kitchen refrigerator. Soon after, the cops drove us to a hospital emergency room, where my wife was treated."

Dr. McKinnon's seriousness, his gravity in retelling the events, his manner, his appearance, remind me of movies I've seen about Abraham Lincoln. Reporter Jill Porter nudges me when he is finished testifying and says, "This is a piece of Renaissance life that the McKinnons are showing us. Neither laughs nor smiles. I can't imagine them tying one on."

Tinari's first question on cross-examination is whether the doctor knew that Knight was bisexual.

"It never entered my mind, whether he was bi or whether he pursued gay relationships."

"Did Knight become intoxicated on the evening that he was killed?"

"No."

"How about you?"

"John is not stingy with his alcohol and I am not stingy in my drinking. I was as rational as I generally am."

In dry, academic tones, he explains that his wife fell asleep not as a result of the alcohol, but "it's characteristic of her behavior. She passed out while the three of us were together—with her head on my lap."

"Did you pass out?"

"I wouldn't use that term. When I got to the guest room, I fell into a deep sleep and heard no noise until I was awakened by my wife."

He acknowledges to Tinari that he later told the police that he had been drunk, "which is a loose way of describing my condition when I'm drinking a lot. I don't mean 'falling down, slurring my speech' drunk. I mean that when my wife woke me, I had a headache, my mouth was dry, and I felt foggy from little sleep.''

McKinnon is dismissed. It is the last I am to see of him. Before leaving Philadelphia, however, he and Rosemary dine with Fitzpatrick's assistant, who raises an interesting point. The young man says to McKinnon, "You're an analyst. You've known John Knight ten years. I don't understand. You must have at least suspected him of being gay."

To which McKinnon replies, "You don't psyche out your friends."

That same day, I drop a note to the doctor at his New Haven address requesting an interview. On June 6, he replies.

"Mrs. McKinnon and I have given your letter careful thought. Having read your article in the *Village Voice*, sent to us by friends, I do not doubt your integrity, your sensitivity, or your interest in the truth in this tragedy. Nevertheless, we have decided to refuse your request for interviews on the subject of John Knight. For while we have no objection particularly to anyone's writing on his life and death, we also have no particular interest or enthusiasm about it, nor do we wish to participate in such an endeavor. The digesting of this raw and unpalatable experience we will do in private; we are not prepared at this point to ruminate publicly."

Court breaks for the weekend.

I return to New York, and dash off a column about the glamour-entrenched opening of *That's Entertainment—Part 2*, finishing it with an interview with former movie diva Kathryn Grayson. Kathryn, a teetotaler, complains that Donald O'Connor and Johnny Weissmuller imbibed on the L.A.-to-New York jet, the naughty boys. She tells me that she was the great love of Howard Hughes's life and that Shirley Temple broke up one of her marriages. More than anything, Grayson wants to retain the title of Miss Chili Queen, which the Charles Kitchen people had bestowed upon her last year. "I make the best chili in California," she boasts. "One day, you'll have a taste."

It's all so unreal. Or is it too real? I'm having problems with conflicting realities.

Monday morning. Back in Philadelphia and the high-ceilinged courtroom with the Corinthian marble columns, for the second week of the Salvatore Soli trial.

Dr. Robert Catherman, the deputy medical examiner who performed the autopsy on Knight's body, takes the stand. He testifies that there were numerous bruises on Knight's face, shoulders, and upper arms that could have been caused by a blunt instrument or fist. The doctor's description of the wounds seems to substantiate what I expect will be D.A. Fitzpatrick's theory that Knight was tortured by Maleno, Melendez, and Soli before the actual stabbing took place.

Sal is dressed in a gray suit today. He wears a tie. If understatement is to win him the sympathy of the jurors, he's finally playing it right. Even his hair is slicked down. And his face is emotionless. As Dr. Catherman vividly describes the condition of the corpse, it is impossible to read what is on Soli's mind. And we still have not heard him utter a word.

His mother, though, tilts her head and slumps forward in her chair, more so than usual. She looks pastier, puffier, than she did last week. Obviously, she is in agony. She's dressed in a faded, sleeveless old dress—a shroud of despair. Her eyes are soft and far away, hands folded in lap—a large watch with a leather band on her left wrist, a diamond wedding ring on her third finger left hand. Atop her little bulldog face is a short crop of gray hair. Mr. and Mrs. Soli sit side by side in the second row of the courtroom. They occupy the same pew each day. Out of respect, no outsider claims the space. It is on the same side of the room in which Sal Soli waits for the decision that will affect all their lives.

Following the medical examiner's report, Fitzpatrick introduces several technical experts, each of whom testifies for the prosecution. An authority on fingerprints reveals that he has examined the rifle, knife, and harpoon gun, and found no identifiable fingerprints. A criminologist claims that there were human blood stains on the rifle and the hunting knife, but there was no blood on the scuba knife. All blood samples taken at Knight's apartment were type O. Type O bloodstains were also found on Melendez's shirt and dungarees.

The last professional to appear as a witness is a chemist who reports that type O blood was discovered on Melendez's coat as well as the fur collar of the garment.

Curiosity gets the best of me. I corner Fitzpatrick after the court breaks for lunch and ask if he intends to call Linda Mary Wells to the stand.

"We don't know where she is. We can't find her."

I start to ask him about Donna DePaul but he gestures to his mouth, signaling that his lips are sealed, courtesy of the gag order. My anxiety pangs about Donna DePaul are quickly quieted. She is called as the next witness for the prosecution.

Donna's persona is a day-and-night contrast to that of Rosemary McKinnon. She's almost a stereotype of the gum-chewing broad trying to act refined. Donna is dressed in a white suit. Her fingernails are devoid of polish. Her hair is short and platinum. Light lipstick. No rouge. It's as if she's hollering, "Look at me, I'm pure," but softness is a quality she carries only on the outside. Her eyes are cold. And her mouth line, which slants down, can't hide the fact that she's a cookie who doesn't smile much.

"How well do you know Salvatore Soli?" asks Fitzpatrick.

"Very well," she answers, in a tone that implies "as if you didn't know."

Under Fitzpatrick's careful tutelage, she offers her version of the events that took place at Joe Paolucci's house on the evening that Knight was murdered. There are slight variations, but her story doesn't differ greatly from accounts given by others who were there.

"We were doing drugs," she admits. "Meth. It's like an upper. You put it in a spoon, water it, then you put it in a syringe. Sal administered it to us. Twice. The second time was after 1 A.M. Felix was the only one not to receive a second shot."

Almost from memory, she recites the litany of the night: Melendez claims that he has a rich friend, the telephone call Melendez makes to Knight, Melendez gets dressed up "real pretty" and leaves Joe Paolucci's place at 3:30 A.M. accompanied by Soli and Maleno.

"I stayed in the kitchen with Linda and Joe and played cards while they were gone.

"About 7 A.M., Sal phoned the house," she continues, "and asked us to pick up Stevie and him at Fifteenth and Shunk Streets. So we drove to that corner. Steve and Sal got into the car with us when we got there. I asked them, 'Where's Felix?' They said, 'That stupid kid got us into a lot of trouble. We could have gotten anything we wanted from that John guy if it weren't for Felix.'

"They told me to pick up Sal's car, which he had parked at a little street near Rittenhouse Square. Joe took Stevie and Sal back to his place. I got Sal's car, and drove back to Paolucci's house on my own. Linda wasn't with us. She didn't come with us.

"When I got there, they were all in the kitchen. Stevie Maleno was wiping off his black leather coat with a dish towel. There was jewelry, coins and things all over the table. Sal claimed the stuff came from Knight's apartment. He was looking at it and separating things. He said, 'Check all this stuff. It's worth a fortune.' Some of it had the initials JK engraved. And there was a gold bracelet with the word 'John' inscribed. Sometime later, Sal took a nail file and scraped the name off.

"While we were still at Joe's house, Sal told me to call the Dorchester and ask for John Knight. The operator said there was trouble in his apartment and that there were cops up there.

"When I related this to Sal, he suggested we all start packing. He said we had to get out of Philadelphia. All the stuff from the table, he pulled together. Then he, Stevie, Linda and me got into Sal's car and headed toward a motel in Jersey."

At 9 A.M., on Sunday, December 7, at the Bo-Bet Motel, Donna carefully scrutinized what was left of the stolen goods: two sets of cuff links, two watches, a necklace, lot of rings with stones in them, a gold bracelet, and coins.

By midafternoon, Felix Melendez arrived at the motel accompanied by Joe Paolucci. Sal immediately pounced on Felix, demanding to know why he stabbed Knight.

"Not whether, but why," affirms Donna.

Sal jumped on top of him and said, "You did kill Knight. You did kill Knight."

Later, she and Sal went to the Rickshaw Restaurant, where they conferred with an attorney. And later still, she joined Maleno for dinner. Then she and Steve Maleno met "the guy who Stevie always bought meth from. Stevie sold this guy some chopped-up soap in a piece of paper wrapped in an envelope. The man thought he was buying meth. He paid Stevie three hundred dollars.''

Donna relates that when she and Steve returned to the Bo-Bet, Felix was still there. He was sitting on the couch, desolate, holding a rag to his head.

"What happened?" cried Donna.

Linda replied that earlier Stevie had sliced Felix with a knife.

"Sal called for a conference," says Donna. "He and Stevie and Joe Paolucci went to another room and shut the door. They stayed there for about twenty minutes. Linda, Felix, and me were in the main room. I didn't talk to Felix. Neither did Linda."

Donna states that they all watched the 11 P.M. news. It showed footage of Knight's apartment, and of Knight's body being carried from the Dorchester on a stretcher. Viewing the grim scene and hearing the sanctimonious voice of the broadcaster as he articulated each gory detail compounded their fears and hammered home the reality of their plight.

They decided to move again. "Me and Sal got into Sal's car," says Donna. "It was the same car I picked up near the Dorchester. Linda and Stevie were in the back seat. Joe Paolucci was driving the other car, with Felix sitting next to him. We drove around New Jersey in an area where there were no homes: Sal's vehicle leading, Joe Paolucci's car behind. At one point, Sal handed Stevie the little revolver and told him to 'keep it quiet.'

"We proceeded some distance. Sal stopped his car, and Joe pulled up alongside. Then Stevie left our car and hopped into Joe's."

A wrinkle—a decided wrinkle—in Donna's testimony. A wrinkle about who was in what car and when. I assume details will be ironed out later. There's also a wrinkle about Felix's murder. No mention. Completely left out. Does Donna think she's auditioning for *Peter Pan*?

She skips to "We went to a gas station and left Sal's auto there. All of us piled in with Joe. All of us except Felix. Stevie said, 'I feel relaxed now. I'm glad we got rid of him.' We went back to the motel. And everyone went to sleep."

The rest of the journey, including the trip to Florida, is outlined by Donna in terms that pretty well parallel the trail detailed by Linda Mary Wells in her confession. Donna adds that she was with Soli when he sold Knight's gold bracelet and two pairs of cuff links at a Miami arcade for two hundred dollars. He used the name Dominick Sofia. She saw him sign that name in the jeweler's register.

Fitzpatrick thanks his star witness for her testimony. Judge Williams calls a break before Tinari takes his scalpel to her. So it's back to the corridors.

One of the reporters points out Donna's mother, who is hovering in the hallway puffing a cigarette, unaware that the man she's standing next to is Felix Melendez's brother, Elias. A few feet from them is an attorney representing the Knight family interests. And no more than three yards in front of him sits Sal's mother in her wheelchair. She is sobbing. Loudly. Mary, her blond daughter, puts Kleenex under Mrs. Soli's nose. She says, "Mama, Mama," and begins crying too. I go over to Mrs. Soli. I want to ask if I can help. I'm tempted to tell her that everything will be all right. But I'm not sure that it will be, and I'm afraid that I may break out in tears too. I do nothing, and return to the courtroom.

"How long have you been using drugs?" asks Tinari, pacing in front of the jurors' box, right fist clenched under his chin.

"I've been using methedrine for about three years," answers Donna.

"Do you have a drug habit?"

"No. I used it when I felt like it. I started doing meth when I was seventeen. The last time I shot up was in Florida. During the last few months, I made a decision to take no drugs at all. I think I hurt my mother enough."

"Did your mother not know you were taking drugs?"

"She didn't know. I kept it away from her. She knew when I was arrested."

Tinari doesn't let her go. It seems that he's out to discredit Donna's testimony by proving that she's an addict. He sermonizes like a Southern Baptist preacher on a TV talk show. He scowls when Donna remarks that methedrine is not a "bad" drug. He demands to know if it leaves track marks. Donna responds that it does, but she has no track marks now. Tinari asks her to show her arm to the court. Donna obediently sheds her white jacket, rolls up the sleeve of her blouse, and points a finger to the big vein of her right arm where the meth had been injected. The jurors collectively strain their necks for a peek.

Tinari increases his pecking. He asks Donna if she wasn't lying about presently taking meth so as to protect her mother.

"Things are all out in the open. Why should I lie?"

"Did you need drugs?"

"I never needed drugs. I wanted them."

"And it would be correct to say that through most of your life between the ages of seventeen and twenty, you were high and then sleeping, high and then sleeping. Is that correct?"

"Yes. That would be correct."

Tinari paces back and forth. He is seething as he switches the line of questioning to Donna's relationship with Soli. He asks her to define it.

"We were girl friend and boy friend—if you wanna put it that way—for about two weeks."

By now, Donna is very much on the defensive and snapping retorts before Tinari has finished wording his questions, which are really veiled accusations when they're not direct accusations. She sits with her hands clasped together atop her purse. Sometimes, they're clasped in front of her crotch, as though she were protecting it. Smart girl. Quick mouth. I wonder what would have befallen Donna had she been born in an upper-class environment.

"How did you feel about Soli?"

"I did what he told me to. I had feelings for him. I liked him. I didn't love him. I don't love nobody."

"Did you like him well enough to go to Florida with him?"

"Yeah."

Suddenly, there's a disruption. Soli's brother, Anthony, enters the courtroom holding a cigarette in one hand and a bouquet of flowers in the other. Judge Williams stops the proceedings and reprimands Anthony.

"They're for my mother because she's so upset," snarls Anthony.

The judge asks him to put out his cigarette and to leave the courtroom until he can behave properly.

I follow Anthony outside. He is fuming, cursing Judge Williams, cursing Nino Tinari, calling the trial a farce, a setup. One of the women waiting outside asks if she can take my place in court. She offers ten dollars and is being pushy about it. While I'm fending her off, Anthony runs in the direction of Mayor Rizzo's sanctuary, screaming, "Sons of bitches, bastards, cocksuckers!"

Apparently the noise doesn't carry into the courtroom. I return to my seat next to Jill Porter and listen

intently as Tinari states that charges against Donna
DePaul were dropped in Philadelphia as part of a deal
made with the D.A.'s office: the other part being that
Donna would testify against Soli. Tinari demands that
the court rule a mistrial.

Calling his bluff, Judge Williams says to Donna,
"Did you have a letter sent to the judge? More
specifically, this judge? Did you have anyone send a
letter to this judge?"

To each of his questions, Donna belts a firm no. So
the wounded Tinari continues to press Donna about her
relationship with Soli, about her tacit disapproval of
Linda Mary Wells, but Donna holds firm like one of
those mechanized dolls: self-sufficient, self-motivated,
and self-preserving. Her speech grows less ladylike
under pressure. It's now sprinkled generously with
dead-end-kid inflections. Each time Tinari tries to trip
her, the crust toughens, and the street smarts rush to the
surface.

And Tinari tries to trip her. Point by point, he
ridicules her testimony. He asks if she got "a little twist
in the stomach—an Italian twist, if you will—when
Linda Mary Wells went 'all the way,' sexually, with
Soli."

"Yes, I did," she replies.

He asks if Linda was actually getting under her skin.

"Yes, she was."

How many beds were there in each of the motels that
they visited?

"At least two."

Were Sal and Linda doing it in front of her?

"Yes. Sal was making love to Linda in my presence
and I was getting upset."

The sequence of events is rehashed from the moment
she entered Joe Paolucci's house until the time that she

and Sal were arrested in Miami. Although a detail is changed here and there, Donna does not alter the substance of her original testimony.

We learn that Sal wore a Sagittarius necklace she had given him. And that Sal had given her a silver watch and ring. Prior to Sal, Donna had been the girl friend for five years of a drug pusher known as Joe the Rat. She had been arrested by the feds in November 1974 for selling meth to an F.B.I. agent and had been given three years on probation.

When Donna is finished, it's as if she has spilled out the most intimate details of her life to a roomful of strangers. But do we know her? Do we know whether she was a good little girl? Did she have Teddy bears and coloring books? Did she go to Catholic schools? What were her hobbies? Will this new notoriety hurt her? Will friends run away because she's squealed on an old beau? Does she have a boy friend now? Or is she alone?

The state rests its case.

Fuck the gag order. "There's no concrete evidence for first-degree murder," Tinari tells reporters. "The evidence for second-degree is not sufficient enough. There's no evidence that Soli assaulted John Knight or Rosemary McKinnon. No evidence of burglary. Nothing here to show that Soli meant to burglarize prior to entry."

Will Soli take the stand tomorrow?

"We'll see."

Will the diaries be entered as evidence?

"No."

Why?

"No comment."

Will Joe Paolucci testify for the defense?

"No comment."

Any further comment on anything?

"The weather is beautiful outside."

Bums lounge outside the theatre. The marquee has a thousand or so yellow bulbs circling it, flashing on and off, twinkle, twinkle, round and round. TROC BURLESQUE, proclaims the sign, as if anyone might miss it. "World's Biggest. Best Hottest Girl Show Ever. See It All. In Total Nude. Adults Only."

At the ticket window, a dignified woman—somebody's mother or aunt, moonlighting—says I can't see the manager: he's working the lights. I pay the tab and enter the almost empty house. America's Sweetheart is peeling to the strains of "Someday My Prince Will Come."

Her hair is blond and frizzy. So is her body. A ratty fur is draped around her shoulders. Provocatively, she slides it down her back to her ass, then throws it to the wings. Off comes a rhinestone necklace. Off come the gloves. She feels her boobs, leans forward, pouts her lips, and offers her tits to the two dozen men in the audience. A couple of them whistle. The dress goes next. What there is of it. Drops to the floor. Now we have a black slip. Cheerful prancing up and down stage. Much caressing of hips. Undulating. "You're doing it too fast," yells a connoisseur. "Not fast enough," yells another. Doesn't matter. Art is art and America's Sweetheart will serve the muse as she sees fit. She jerks her pelvis forward and executes a dazzling bump. Look of Cloud Nine on her face. Off goes the slip. "More." "More." She writhes on the floor. Off go the panties.

I ask a peon with a flashlight to show me to the light booth.

"Can't."

I tell him I'm a member of the press and need to see the manager.

"He's not here."

I ask him if he knows Linda Mary Wells.

"Sure."

"Do you know where I can find her?"

"The cops were asking that same question. She danced here a couple of months ago. Sweet kid. Can't help you."

"Can you tell me what she was like?"

"Yeah. She was looking for a father. That's what she was like."

"When will the manager return?"

"He's in and out. In and out. He can't tell you nothing I can't tell you."

On my way out, I say "thanks for nothing" to the cashier.

"Didn't you see the manager?"

"No. The usher wouldn't let me near the light booth."

"What does the usher look like?"

I describe him.

"You were talking to the manager."

The detective suggests that I stay away from headquarters. He asks where I'm calling from. I tell him I'm at a phone booth near the Troc. I also tell him who my contact is. He says he's been waiting for my call. I know this is as close as I'm going to get to the diaries.

An hour later, he picks me up in front of City Modeling Studios, which is on the same block as the Troc. I recognize him immediately: he's been around the courtroom since the start of the trial. He recognizes me, too. He beckons me into his car. Cramped in the back seat is a dog of unspecified breed, probably a bastard relative of the family that carries whiskey to lost skiers in the Alps. The animal is either on Valium or three steps from death. It hardly moves. The detective calls it Ruth. The clump looks like a Ruth. Definitely not watchdog material.

Ruth and I have something in common: neither of us stirs as the detective drives us to an area of Philadelphia completely alien to me. He pulls to a stop, pats Ruth's head, and says, "We won't be long, girl." The detective and I enter a restaurant decorated in early Sigmund Romberg. We take a corner booth.

"Let's talk about the diaries," I say.

"Let's look at the menu first," he says.

We order scotch straight, and settle for Wiener schnitzel. The drinks take a long time in coming.

"What specifically do you want to know?"

"Everything. Were the entries daily?"

"Daily for maybe a week or two period. Then Knight would stop for three. Then there'd be Saturday, Sunday, Monday—that kind of thing. Some of the entries were short. Like 'Start working more.' 'Start straightening things out.' Most of them were about feelings. He'd write about sex, reacting positively to a good sexual encounter with a woman. That would make him happy. But then he'd write about a homosexual experience, and he'd write with obviously more . . ."

"Soul-searching?" I offer.

"No. Not soul-searching. If he had a really terrific homosexual experience, he'd describe it in much more glowing kinds of enjoyment terms. The description of heterosexual relationships that were successful, I guess, made him proud, or bootstrapped him into a sense of 'I'm on the right road now.' And yet, the homosexual experiences were more fulfilling to him in the standpoint of emotions."

"Were they strictly blow jobs, pardon the expression?"

The detective laughs. He's handsome when he laughs. He's handsome when he doesn't laugh. "The expression

is pardoned,'' he says. "In polite circles we call it
fellatio. No. Not strictly blow jobs at all, although blow
jobs seemed to be, according to Knight's entries, the
most titillating experience of all.''

"Done to him?''

"No. That he did.''

"Fascinating.''

"Yeah. Fellatio that he did.''

The detective gets away from the Knight case for a
few moments and tells me about the kind of work in
which he specializes. He is direct and unassuming, and
I'm leery about why he's offering his time and sharing
his knowledge: giving me information that no more
than a dozen people are privy to. I'm flattered when he
says that he knows my work, and that our mutual friend
said I could be trusted. For some reason, though, I feel I
must be flip and fresh to this perfectly nice man: more
than I usually am. I ask him if he's a closet detective.
The remark gets no response. It deserves a slap in the
face. He orders another round of drinks. I tell the waiter
to put everything on one bill. I'll pay the check. It's
called guilt.

"Did Knight discuss his homosexuality at length in
the diaries?''

"He talked about homosexual experiences and how
euphoric he had been in a particular homosexual encounter, but he wouldn't say that homosexuality itself is
terrific. It was a disease that one overcomes, rather than
accepts as part of one's makeup. I know for people like
you it's fine, but for this poor guy, it was death. It is
fine with you, isn't it?''

"It's fine with me.''

"Now I didn't read that much of Knight's Detroit entries when he was really heavy into his analysis because I
was looking for things relative to Philadelphia and the
six to twelve months before he came to Philadelphia.

But in the pages I read, there was a tremendous amount about Billy Sage. Knight couldn't get him out of his head. The entries on Billy waxed and waned—like a typical love affair. They are fascinating, but difficult to read.''

He starts picking at his meat and orders wine for both of us. Under the table his leg rubs against mine and I try not to bestow motivations. But I'm aware of it. Boy, am I aware of it.

"Christ," he says. "I don't know how many hours, how many days I spent going through letters and a lot of stuff unrelated to the diaries before I even started on the diaries. There were letters from some kid in London. And souvenirs of Billy Sage.''

"Why isn't Billy in Philadelphia for the trial? Do you know if he's still in Detroit?''

"He is.''

"Surviving?''

"I guess so. His wife is painting red, white, and blue flags on women's fingernails for the Bicentennial. She's a manicurist at some suburban beauty parlor.

"Bringing John Knight up to Billy Sage is not a very pleasant subject," he discloses. "John was taking very good care of Billy and Billy had a juvenile idea of what the death of Knight was going to bring him. It brought him absolutely nothing. He's pissed off that he didn't get his lollipop when he expected to.

"But back to the diaries. Knight's Philadelphia entries stated that he'd pick up kids off the street, but that he also had pimps. The pimps were supplying him with both guys and girls. There are a number of encounters he had with whores. I mean, out-and-out first-class five-dollar-a-night hookers, like the type you don't see in nice family restaurants like this.''

"Would he pick up female hookers from the street, too?''

"Sometimes. But mostly it was phone calls to whomever. Felix Melendez supplied him with a couple of girls. The girl-hooker thing, I guess, didn't bother Felix when it came to Knight. The boy-hooker thing obviously did. Think about the whole bit. Here was Knight, a guy in a position to buy anybody with class. He didn't want that. He didn't want that because he realized that a high-class prostitute would know what he was. He took the position that if he got a slut, he could look on her with disdain, even if she realized that he preferred boys."

I'm suddenly more aware of the detective's leg than I am of his words because it's practically welded to mine. I don't move away. In fact, I press. "Hey," he asks. "Are you coming on to me?" I emit a slight groan, and ask if there was anything in the diaries to indicate that Knight showed off his money and position when he was with these whores.

"No indication in the diaries," he responds. "But I know that one of his methods was showering these people with money and gifts, the kind of thing that led to the Felix Melendez problem.

"What's interesting to me," he adds, "is that John Knight and I were about the same age. How old are you?"

I tell him, but knock off four years.

"I can really relate to what Knight was going through on the age thing. The whole traditional identity problem that the average Joe has when he turns thirty. That's the time when you think, I've got to hurry up and do all these things while I'm still twenty-nine, because when I'm thirty I won't be able to."

"I remember it well," I sigh, lying through my teeth. "Except with me, I want to cram in everything before every birthday."

"Maybe that's why you're a reporter. Always dissatisfied."

"Not always."

"Too bad you're not a woman."

"Too bad you're a cop."

With that, our leg stranglehold breaks. I should have stayed an extra year at finishing school. Anyway, I suggest that we return again to our deceased friend's diary.

"Getting back," he says. "Getting back again to John Knight, when he turned thirty, everything continued on, the world didn't end, and he saw that it wasn't a traumatic change. The sky didn't fall on Chicken Little."

"The sky fell in a different way," I answer. "Totally and absolutely."

"You know he was an alcoholic?"

"I know."

Two women enter. They're led to a booth, and my dinner-partner informant says, "Christ, I know one of them. Let's change seats, I can't risk being seen with you."

We switch seats. He's a tiny bit tipsy now, and knocks over my glass of wine as he places his Hart, Schaffner and Marx-tailored frame in a chair with his back toward them.

"I don't think she'll recognize me. Dated her once, before I got married."

I don't ask him if Ruth is his wife. That's too bitchy. Instead, I go back to John's drinking. Was he definitely an alcoholic?

"Definitely. He very often wrote when he was drunk. He very often talked about how much he had to drink before he wrote. There were several Philadelphia entries that were almost unintelligible from the standpoint of the quality of the writing, because he was drunk. Most of the time when he wrote his diaries, he had been drinking.

"When he was drunk, he'd often go out to Rittenhouse Square or Spruce Street and pick up some kid. He'd wake up the next morning and give the guy a hundred dollars and tell him to get lost. Melendez was never fully accepting of that from the start. He didn't like the idea of being rejected that way. Melendez tried to make contact with him. Basically, John didn't want to have anything to do with him. In his sober or lucid moments, John was ashamed of Melendez. That offended the kid. I'm not saying that that motivated Melendez to intentionally go out and get John Knight. But if you accept the proposition that Melendez killed John Knight, it explains the rage which would instill in Melendez the urge to kill."

"You were in Knight's apartment. You worked on the case," I say. "Since they won't be bringing it up in court, can you tell me exactly what was found in Knight's foot locker?"

"About three hundred dollars' worth of pornographic books and commercial movies, the eight-millimeter variety. None of it was homemade, in the sense that it was filmed by John Knight. It was the stuff you buy in pornographic shops. A lot of hard-core pornographic books, most of them homosexual. Somewhat ironically, some old childhood books. The Hardy Boys kind of books that a kid has when he's ten. And the diaries."

"Any toys?"

"Some were found, but not in the foot locker. They were found in suitcases piled up next to the door. It looked like somebody intended to haul the sex toys out of there as part of the loot. In one of the suitcases was a couple of double-ended dildoes. No leather or whips or handcuffs or cat-o'-nine-tails.

"Different people take different views about Knight's apartment. I maintain that you could visit his place and never know that it was the home of a homosexual. Maybe I'm not sophisticated enough to know."

"Get off it. You're too sophisticated."

"Thanks. Other people have said you could tell it was a homosexual's quarters from the artwork. There was a Japanese print in one of the bathrooms—an explicit sexual scene. Some detectives concluded, from the painting, that the guy liked men. I remember going through the apartment with a couple of cops and they were examining the ceiling very closely to check if there had ever been a mirror on it. It tickled the hell out of me. Totally unrealistic. Sure, there were mirrors in the gymnasium where he worked out—but what does that tell? One of our men thought he might have another pad somewhere. A 'trick' apartment. No such thing.

"Knight's apartment got a good thorough overhaul. After sifting through his possessions, I realized that there was no damn underwear, anywhere. I said, 'Wait a minute. This is not real.' Then we found out that most of Knight's stuff was at the laundry."

"He did wear underwear?"

"Yeah." He grins. "Doesn't everybody? Do you?"

I don't answer. "Do you?"

He doesn't answer, either, but I can see he does.

Nino Tinari announces that there will be no witnesses for the defense. He claims that there should be no adverse inference made from Salvatore Soli's failure to testify. Soli, in silence, is saying, "I'm not guilty." He is pleading "not guilty" on all counts.

● ● ●

Jurors shuffle as a bloc into the courtroom. Bodies
plop into assigned seats. Signs of weariness are evident.
How long can one stay cooped up without contact with
the outside world? It's now a week. Granted, the jurors
have been shown a decent time during their period of
sequestration: the hotel where they dwell is modest, the
restaurants where they eat are good. Undoubtedly,
they've gotten to know each other well. Some may continue their friendships after the trial is over. After all,
they have a murder case in common. It has brought
them all together. But now, in the confines of the
courtroom, they are silent. Depersonalized. The arche-
typical jury.

Nino Tinari faces them, and it's corn-pone time down
Pennsylvania way as he presents his closing argument.

"You people are from all walks of life, from all areas
of Philadelphia," he begins. "The quality of your
honesty made us select you and you and you. . . ." He
salutes each juror like Queen Elizabeth waving at the
peasants from her royal coach. "Yes, this is the Bicentennial year. Yes, we talk about the rights of all
America. Yes, you epitomize all America. Yes, when
you took that oath, you made a promise to have an open
mind. Yes, you took an oath signed with the blood of
the Civil War, World War I and World War II. Yes,
even the Vietnam War."

His rhetoric is awful. It this were vaudeville, he'd be
hooked off the stage.

"John Knight is gone. It's not your duty to seek
vengeance. This case is not to be determined by the
heart. It must be determined by the mind. We must
presume that Salvatore Soli is innocent. . . ."

Soli wears a subdued gray business suit today. He is
the picture of innocence. Proper. Tranquil. For support, the entire Soli family is in court, except brother
Anthony, who apparently has had it.

"Salvatore Soli has a shroud of innocence over his head," continues Tinari. "If there is only one thread of that shroud remaining on his shoulders, he must be found innocent."

On the subject of reasonable doubt, Tinari emphasizes that "it is based on evidence or the lack of evidence." His two hands are perched on the jury box's walnut rail: fingers perfectly manicured, cuffs—about four inches' worth—peek out from under the sleeves of his loud tan and brown jacket. This is his third appearance in that suit. Plaid pants with razor-sharp crease. Shiny black shoes, with heels just a little higher than those manufactured by Florsheim. Probably custom built. They underline Tinari's shortness. No question about how dynamic he is. Or how persistent—like a used-car salesman. But is the jury buying? The seven women and five men sit stone-faced.

District Attorney Fitzpatrick, meanwhile, scans the room. His hands cover his mouth, *à la* Soli. Fitzpatrick is fidgety. He removes his horn-rimmed glasses and places them on the table in front of him. He pats the back of his head, scratches his right eyebrow, jots down notes, whispers to his assistant, crosses and uncrosses his legs.

Am I dreaming, or is Salvatore Soli the calmest person in the courtroom?

Tinari fires a four-gun blast at Donna DePaul. "That testimony comes from a corrupt source," he says. "You cannot twist corruptness, which is badness, into something called goodness."

Referring to Soli's escape to Florida, he spurts, "Flight is not evidence of guilt." Then he takes us on a trip down memory lane. "Rosemary McKinnon? No finer individual have I seen testify in many, many a year. Dr. McKinnon? Equally as fine." To stress their fineness, Tinari reminds us that they were drunk. He concludes that "No one can castigate them for having a few drinks.

"John Knight had alcohol in him, too. Yet that phone call meant something to Knight. You've got to form an inference. Isn't it strange, ladies and gentlemen, that at three o'clock in the morning, John Knight didn't want to go to bed? The phone call meant he was ready for a good time. Didn't matter whether it was a boy or girl. Juices began to flow.

"What about Melendez? How was Melendez going to dress on his visit to John Knight's apartment? Donna DePaul sees Melendez get dressed. She sess him put on white gloves. Isn't that indicative of something effeminate?

"And what about the scene at Knight's apartment? Melendez walks in. No busting in. Of course, we know that Dr. McKinnon was wiped out. During the time Salvatore Soli spent with Mrs. McKinnon, she is not touched by him. Rosemary McKinnon, with all her degrees. She is not infallible.

"With Soli out of the apartment, who do we have left? Only Melendez and Rosemary McKinnon. Melendez in an apartment he's familiar with, with people who have been drinking. When one is drunk, one becomes a weakling. One doesn't need to be a bionic man to push over a drunk."

In argument after argument, Tinari reiterates that Knight's murder had been carried out by Melendez after Soli had withdrawn from the apartment.

"Salvator Soli had nothing to do with it. You can't attribute first-degree murder to him."

Sometimes Tinari sounds like a rabbi at a memorial service singing the praises of a humanitarian who has just left this earth, sometimes he looks as if he's about to get down on one knee and sing "Mammy." I half expect the oil painting of Justice, which hangs over Judge

Williams's podium, to drop to the floor.

"Think of that cliché, Familiarity breeds contempt," oozes Tinari in his best corn-syrup voice. "I wonder if that emotion of contempt began to swell up when Melendez saw Knight." Tinari's arms flail, then they creep into his jacket pocket. The performance grows. It is so outrageous that one wonders if today's fledgling attorney takes dancing lessons? Body movement? Studies voice? Do the top-drawer lawyers go to the Actors Studio?

Tinari pounds the jurors' rail with his fist. "You can't attribute first-degree murder to Salvatore Soli. Don't allow your emotions to play havoc with you. Don't forget your intellect and be ruled by your heart."

He pauses. Then he mentions Donna DePaul's name in a whisper. "Does an individual who places her hand on the Bible tell the truth? What interests, motives, biases, what benefits, what detriments, does Donna DePaul have in testifying? Was there an ulterior motive in her testimony?

"Donna. Yes. Donna. Twenty years of age, but I'll bet each and every one of you that she's seen more in her twenty years than all of us put together. Donna. A woman scourged. Hell hath no fury as a woman scourged."

Under her breath, Marilyn Schaeffer of the *Bulletin* asks me if that's anything like a woman scorned? Or is it like a woman purged?

"What about Donna's interests?" continues Tinari. "If you put her interest in a saving account . . . if you could change that interest into money, Donna DePaul would be a wealthy woman. Donna. Yes. We're talking about a child who's been caught in the net. Worldly wise, sexually wise. A girl who knows more than a twenty-year-old knows.

"Don't be fooled by the manner in which she dressed

on the stand—as if she were driven here in the snow in pristine purity. Don't they do it sweetly, the Commonwealth? Don't they do it just at the proper season? A girl who has been on a meth trip since the age of seventeen. One who has been high"—Tinari's arms wave high—"and sleeping." Tinari's arms sink toward the floor. He repeats the words and gestures and it is difficult not to guffaw. Is this what the judicial system is about? It's hard enough for a juror to sift through facts, nonfacts, and evidence without having the intrusion of schtick.

"Donna. When it's convenient for her, she remembers words. When it isn't, she forgets. You've got to scrutinize those words. You've got to put those words under a colored glass."

Having hinted that the McKinnons are drunks, having attempted to discredit Donna, Tinari next lashes out at the press. He calls the case "one of the most celebrated to hit Philadelphia in years. It is celebrated because the individual himself—John Knight—was in newspapers. It is celebrated because the press made it a *cause célèbre.*"

In conclusion, Tinari bows his head as in prayer. "Salvatore Soli's fate is in you hands," he murmurs. "Isn't it strange that we collect twelve people to determine his life? Well, that isn't so strange, because two thousand years ago, there were twelve people who selected the fate of mankind."

The jurors continue to look deadpan. There isn't a wet eye in the house.

District Attorney Fitzpatrick's turn.

"Conspiracy: the act of one person or the act of all. Probably the most important point in this case.

"You must find an agreement between two or more to commit an unlawful act," he tells the jury. "In this case, there were three people and they did agree to commit an unlawful act—to rob John Knight.

"It has been suggested by lawyer Tinari that Soli was part of the conspiracy, but withdrew from it. No dispute. Soli was part of the conspiracy to rob Knight and the McKinnons."

Tinari jumps to his feet. He asks for a mistrial, and continues to demand a mistrial throughout Fitzpatrick's closing argument. Each request is nipped in the bud by Judge Williams. If I read correctly, there's no love lost between the judge and Tinari.

To give him his due, Fitzpatrick does not resort to pyrotechnics. No pacing. No verbal dancing. No archaic use of the English language. No references to Jesus or the Last Supper. With his right hand in his jacket pocket, he stands at the jury box and delivers a sort of Midwestern, good-ole-boy soliloquy. He doesn't exactly pull out the stops for warmth and humaneness. But all the flip he flashed to the reporters in the courtroom corridors has been replaced by a conservative, underplayed demeanor. He is Greer Garson to Tinari's Kay Francis.

"Consider the people involved in this drama," he says. "Whatever John Knight was, he was wealthy. Whatever his social habits or sexual preferences, he came into contact with people who would want to take his wealth from him.

"From that entire holocaust, not one defendant was seen with a mark that Knight might have inflicted. Knight could not have defended himself. The McKinnons survived solely because they didn't panic.

"The scheme originated with Soli. He called each and every shot from the morning of December 7 until he was apprehended. He make the first move: he said he needed money. He had the meth. He did the injecting. He told Melendez to call Knight. He told Melendez to dress better. Soli later laid out the loot. He got Donna to call the Dorchester. He suggested 'we pack up and get away.' He suggested the spot where they went. He got rid of the loot. He called Paolucci and asked him to get Melendez to the hotel. He threatened Melendez. He drove the lead car on Melendez's last journey. He handed the gun—the murder weapon—to Stevie Maleno. It was Soli who did these things.

"Salvatore Soli was the captain of the team. He was the quarterback, the man who made each and every decision, the leader of this band of Vikings wreaking terror all over Rittenhouse Square."

Antoinette Soli's eyes are closed tight as Fitzpatrick talks. Her upper and lower lids grit against each other. If there were some way her husband and children could keep her from going through this daily torture—some way to tie her to her bed at home. Pain emanates from every crevice. Pain that isn't merely physical. Certainly there must be a feeling of guilt. Certainly a sense of "What did I do wrong?" Certainly sorrow for Sal, herself, her husband, her other children. Certainly flashbacks of Salvatore as a baby, as a growing boy, as a young man. Perhaps a flash-forward signaling doom. Perhaps a thought about the other parents. Where are they this afternoon? Is Dorothey Knight following the trial in the warmth of the Columbus, Georgia, home, hearing the events on radio, discussed, dissected, distorted? Is Felix Melendez's mother reading about the case in Puerto Rico? Is she thinking about the last time she saw her son—at the airport in Philadelphia a month before his death? Are they, too, in pain? Or has the pain slowly subsided for them?

"About Melendez, we don't know much," continues Fitzpatrick. "We know he willingly went along with the scheme. We know what happened after the piece of dirty work was done at the Dorchester. We know

Melendez did not admit to killing Knight and Salvatore Soli threatened him with a knife. We know that Stevie Maleno made Melendez dig a hole, called his name, and pumped bullets into his head.

"Melendez was good-looking, slender, and may have had a homosexual relationship with John Knight. If, indeed, they had a relationship, he was the only one who'd have benefitted from Knight being alive. We know that Soli told Rosemary McKinnon, 'We have come to settle a grudge.'

"But we don't know why Knight was killed. We may never know. We know they were looking for money and drugs. Perhaps the grudge came about because John Knight did not have any money or drugs. And when they couldn't find them, they stuck a knife into Knight. They got jewelry—but whatever they got—whatever they got—was that sufficient reason to take a man's life?

"On twelve occasions, they submitted John Knight to either beatings or stabbings. Finally, they opted for things they could take out of his apartment, goods they could turn into quick cash. The silverware was too bulky, so they left the silverware."

Fitzpatrick explains that it would have been virtually impossible for Melendez alone to have moved Knight's body from room to room. He claims that all Melendez wanted to do was to go to the back room to see Knight. He states that Soli and Maleno schemed to put the blame on Melendez, after they had fled the apartment.

"What kind of a man does it take to plunge a knife into a chest and administer other wounds? What we know about Melendez is that in a twenty-story flight down an elevator, all he could do was knick a woman's finger.

"Call it drugs, if you will, but the entire scheme was ill conceived. It was the act of individuals who should know better. Specifically, it was the act of a very arrogant, cocky human being who has no regard for a life—a human being who would kill a man brutally in that man's own apartment.

"There is no reason to believe Knight died as the result of a lovers' quarrel. True, we don't know exactly why he was killed. But we know how he was killed. This is a clearcut case of willful, deliberate, premeditated, well-thought-out murder. Not an act of passon, but an act of torture over the period of time during which Knight's apartment was ransacked.

"You should have very little difficulty deciding that the murder was done with the consent and under the direction of Salvatore Soli. Your verdict should be guilty of all counts and guilty of murder in the first degree."

A couple of minutes after Fitzpatrick finishes his remarks, Mrs. Soli moans and slumps forward in her wheelchair, almost falling to the floor. Her face has turned an ashen white. She makes a fist and clutches her chest. Her breath is labored. Sweat beads erupt on her forehead. She gasps—fighting to catch her breath. Wheeze. Gasp. Wheeze. Gasp.

"Oh, my God," wails her daughter, Mary. "Oh, my God. She's having a heart attack."

Salvatore stands up and strains forward to see. Two officers close in on him. Judge Williams orders the courtroom cleared. As Soli is led past Fitzpatrick's assistant, he sneers, "You fucking bastard." It is the first time Soli's voice is audible in the courtroom.

Mrs. Soli is wheeled past the journalists and onlookers who crowd the corridor. Her body is covered by blankets. Only the tiny tortured face is visible. Her daughter shields her, as if she were the Hope Diamond. In front of the ambulance, a WPVI-TV photographer zeroes in with his camera and Mary Soli whacks him with her purse.

That night, Mrs. Soli is reported in critical condition at Jefferson Hospital.

And that night, I met my florist pal at a bar called Maxine's. I'm early. "Some People" sung by Ethel Merman blasts from the jukebox. Forty men sing along in nasal twang.

"What's your garbage?" asks the bartender. I notice that he's got a well-stocked top shelf: Beefeaters, Pernod, Strega, Ouzo, Tanqueray, chartreuse that looks as if it's used occasionally—no booze of the swamp-water variety. And I notice that everyone's having a good time and almost everyone's past his prime, which gives food for thought about the irony of the gay bar scene. The clubs where the liberated prefer to congregate are dark, dank, unfriendly—places where a stranger wandering in off the street has to have a gimmick such as a performing cobra or a fifteen-inch cock to rate a nod. But the old-fashioned, old-style piano bars, where queens sing gems from *Gypsy* and call each other "pussycat," are usually spots where every toad is made to feel welcome. Maxine's is such a spot, and there will be bars like Maxine's as long as there are homosexuals.

The jukebox stops, the piano player tickles the ivories, and the florist walks in.

"I thought you'd like Maxine's," he says.

"I love it. Reminds me of the only place we had in Montreal when I first came out."

"You fit into everything," he says. "I wish I was like you."

Plop. Here we go again. Better to sing than listen.

"Play 'Street of Dreams,' " I say to the pianist.

"How does it go?"

I hum a few bars.

"Don't know. How about this one?" He breaks into

"Send in the Clowns." Almost everybody breaks into "Send in the Clowns." The florist doesn't.

"I bet John Knight and Felix Melendez never came here," he says. "I bet you really think this is a waste of time because it's not the kind of place Knight and Melendez would go to."

I don't answer.

"I wish I could be as interested in something as much as you are interested in them. I wish I could be promiscuous like you," he says.

"What's bothering you?"

"You're fucking with me, and you're not fucking with me."

"Does that mean I'm promiscuous?"

Silence. He disappears. I go on singing a medley of Garland with three very gay Philadelphians. Midway through "Get Happy," he reappears.

"I just blew a guy in the bathroom," he announces.

"Did you enjoy it?"

Long pause. "No. I did it to see how you'd react."

"Well, I wasn't there. What do you want me to say?"

"I want you to get mad."

I start to get mad. Not at what he did, but at the games he's playing, and I tell him so.

Suddenly, he's singing "Carolina in the Morning." He puts his arms around me and we sway back and forth. And we stay for another half dozen oldies but goodies, then walk the dozen blocks to his house, holding hands on Spruce Street, like we really meant something to each other. And it's real nice.

Back home, we have sex. He plays the aggressor and it's a kind of reversal of identities. By being the penetrator, the autonomy is in his hands. He is the boss, the man. It is more a confirmation of self for him than a loss of self for me. He lets out a primal scream at orgasm, then lies next to me. We cling to each other. He lights a cigarette. The smoke shows his eyes: they're green and distant.

"What are you thinking?" I murmur.

"It's more than a story." He starts to shake. I hold him tight. I ask him what's wrong.

"But it is, isn't it."

"Isn't what."

"More than a story."

"It's a story, and that's all it is. Look, the more I know about them, the better I'll write it. To write something good, you've got to know one hundred times more than what goes down on paper."

"I don't believe you," he says. "I think you've fallen in love."

"I like you. I really do. I like you a lot. You're a good person. I like having sex with you. But I'm not in love with you."

"Not me. Them. My competition is two dead men."

The next morning, I leave his house. And I don't come back again.

Thursday. May 20. The drama is on. The playacting is over. The makeup of the courtroom is different today. None of the regular groupies are here. Student attorneys who have flown in and out of the room like migrant birds are nesting in other chambers, watching other attorneys perform. Mr. Soli and son Anthony aren't around. Mary Soli, who says her mother spent a restful night, is accompanied by yet another Soli sister, one I haven't seen before. The press contingent is down to bone: Jill Porter provides Ju-jubes to the crew. Fitzpatrick is present, of course, sporting a midnight-blue suit, the kind one wears to a funeral. Tinari is in coordinated beige. Soli in powder blue.

At 10:45 A.M., Judge Williams suggests that the jurors get themselves comfortable, instructs them on their duties, and defines the various charges.

"The person accused of the crime does not have to present evidence in his defense," explains the judge in an authoritative, fatherly manner. He expounds on the differences between evidence which a witness relates from his own personal experience, and that which is circumstantial. "You must decide first that the testimony of the witness is accurate. Alone, it may be sufficient to prove a defendant guilty."

Sounds of construction work blast into the room from the courtyard. A cop closes the one window which is open. The American flag can be seen waving in the breeze outside. Fitzpatrick is sipping water as if it were champagne. His pinky sticks up.

"You must not concern yourself with either counsel's objections, or with material stricken from the record," says the judge. "When and if there's a conflict in testimony, you must decide which testimony to believe. You must remember that two or more witnesses to an event may see or hear it differently."

He discusses Donna DePaul's arrest on drug charges. "It's been stated that she received help on matters she had before the court. You must weigh whether she would come before the court and testify truthfully.

"As for Joe Paolucci and Linda Mary Wells, these witnesses were available to both parties. Since they were not called, you must not draw inferences favorable or unfavorable for either side.

"Regarding the evidence on Salvatore Soli fleeing Philadelphia and altering his physical appearance. Generally speaking, when a crime is committed and a person flees, it means that that person is conscious of guilt. He may flee, however, if innocent. Weigh this evidence with all the other evidence presented in this case.''

By reiterating in dulcet tones what we have previously heard from colorful witnesses, the judge puts the jurors into a somnolent state, along with everyone else in the room. Entertainment isn't what the summing up is, but we've already had show business. It is apparent now why those who don't have to stay to the finish don't stay. Which isn't to blame the good judge. Instructing the jurors is part of that system called Justice.

Judge Williams repeats the various degrees of murder. Passion, he concludes, includes anger, terror, rage. If there is passion without reasonable cause or provocation, the verdict is murder, and not voluntary manslaughter.

He orders the jurors to select a foreman. Their verdict must be unanimous. Alternate jurors will be excused when the jury finishes deliberation. Only one count of murder must be found.

At 12:15 P.M., Judge Williams wraps up his summary. The jurors leave the courtroom to discuss the case among themselves for the very first time. Undoubtedly, each will have a lot to say on the fate of the short man in the powder-blue suit, despite the many questions that remain unanswered.

Questions that remain unanswered for me. Why wasn't Joe Paolucci called as a witness for the defense? In his statement to the Philadelphia Homicide Bureau, Paolucci said that Felix Melendez had told him, ''I had to cut the guy.'' Paolucci later told me the same thing. Sal's sister Mary wanted him called. Three times she asked Nino Tinari to use his statement. According to Mary, ''Each time Tinari said the statement wasn't important enough. He said, 'I'm the lawyer.' ''

The medical examiner maintains that two bullets were taken from Felix Melendez's body. Steven Maleno claims that he shot Melendez three times: once straight on, twice after he had fallen to the ground. Linda Mary Wells swears that she heard three shots when she was in the car parked nearby. What happened to the third bullet?

There's also always been a mystery about the gun that was used to kill Melendez. Soli says that he picked it up when he was ransacking Knight's apartment. If it did belong to John Knight, it would have been registered. No one has established that the bullets found in Felix Melendez were fired from a gun owned by Knight.

Formalities done with, the courtroom becomes a rumpus room until the verdict is reached. Marilyn Schaeffer organizes a pool. We're to guess the number of hours the jurors will take to reach their decision, and just what that decision will be. Each reporter throws fifty cents into the kitty. So does Emmet Fitzpatrick. Popular opinion is still manslaughter—and it'll take two to four hours before the verdict is in.

So we hang out.

At three thirty-five, the jurors are brought back. They've written a note to Judge Williams asking him to once again define murder in the first, second, and third degrees. He does so.

At 6 P.M., the judge enters the courtroom, but the jury doesn't. False alarm. He disappears quickly. It's going to be a long wait. Everybody's getting slaphappy. Police guards flirt with reporters. Fitzpatrick plays with reporters. His caustic wit contradicts his somber appearance. I ask him if there's a special courtroom dress code for lawyers.

"The first thing I had to teach my team was how to

dress," he replies. "They used to walk around like Tinari in orange suits and yellow ties."

At seven thirty, a court attendant is asked to fetch Fitzpatrick and Tinari. Tinari can't be found. Fitzpatrick snaps, "He's supposedly at a newsstand, but Nino's probably having a beer or something."

At eight twenty-five, the court reconvenes. All the reporters are back. Soli is brought in. What can he be thinking as the pronouncement of his life is about to take place? If he were to expire of a heart attack, or in an automobile accident, he'd die quickly. If he is sentenced to the electric chair, it's like dying of cancer. A slow process. Appeals. Retrials. Hope of being saved. Uncertainty. Chemotherapy, perhaps administered by a governor somewhere. And then, what? Release? A life in jail?

The jurors file in. The foreman stands. He reads the verdict.

"The jury has found Salvatore Soli guilty of murder in the first degree. Guilty of robbery. Guilty of burglary. Guilty of criminal conspiracy."

Stone silence. Then the sound of Soli's sister sobbing. Then the sight of one of the women jurors crying. Then the rage of Nino Tinari as he demands that the jurors be polled individually.

Soli rises. His hands are locked behind his back. There is a smirk on his face, and it remains there as each juror repeats "Guilty of murder in the first degree." Loud and clear. Again and again.

When the last audible sound of guilty drifts into the air, Soli motions with his right hand to Judge Williams and says, "If it's death, give it to me now."

The hallway is mobbed. The TV camera lights are blinding. Squinting in the glare, five microphones at his

mouth, Tinari blasts Judge Williams for allowing Fitzpatrick to introduce testimony about Melendez's
murder and for permitting the jurors to view slides and
photographs of Knight's body which "aroused
passions. Those jurors should have returned a verdict
that was consistent with the evidence."

Fitzpatrick, surrounded by security guards, claims
that he's glad the trial is over, and calls the verdict
"fair."

Away from the cameras, Mary Soli, her eyes still
watery, says, "I'm sorry. Really sorry. Sal didn't kill
him. There's enough evidence there to prove he didn't
kill him."

The following morning, the jurors return to the courtroom. Their decision is not to give it to Soli now. It is
not death in the electric chair. Merely life imprisonment.

Over. All over. Done with. The jurors file out.

And Vivian Aleica of UPI wins the four dollars in the
reporters' kitty.

"You know, sir, I'll be getting social security in thirty
years—in the year 2006. My whole life stinks. Can you
give me a quarter?"

It's a good gimmick. I give the guy a quarter.
Anyway, he's blocking the entranceway to the Kensington storefront apartment where one of the jurors
lives.

I ring the bell.

"What time is it?" asks the woman who answers.
"I'm just making a transition from a sleeping consciousness to an awakening consciousness."

She invites me in. Tells me to put away the cassette
recorder. Says that the jurors made an agreement

among themselves not to talk to the press. Under no circumstances am I to use her name.

Was she surprised that she was chosen as a juror in the first place?

"Certainly. I'm not that kind of person. I never think of anything heavy. I always ask opinions of others."

Was serving as a juror boring?

"No. But it was like having your whole attention level switched. Sometimes I had insights I wanted to convey. Sometimes I wanted to answer back the lawyers. Like Tinari's twelve-apostle number. So ludicrous. Those attorneys are not truth finders. They're storytellers."

She heads for the stove to boil water for Nescafé and mentions that if it weren't for the fact that I had sat next to her boy friend a couple of times in court, she wouldn't be rapping, and she feels guilty that she is. But, on the other hand, the trial is past history, so why not? But she'd hate to have her fellow jurors guess it was her spilling the beans "because we were a family in a way, with different age groups and from different places in life."

The thing that most upset this woman during the trial was that "once Fitzpatrick held up a knife—the one they found in the exercise room—and I started gagging. It must have been Freudian. When they showed the picture of Knight's hands tied, I noticed he had sensitive hands and I felt bad for him. But most of the time, the emotional thing about his suffering was lost. When you're a juror, you're less concerned with the victim. The torture which was inflicted on Knight registered, but it registered while we were deliberating.

"When we retired into the room to discuss the case, I know that some jurors had already made up their minds, while others hadn't. I was one of the ones who hadn't."

From the back of a kitchen-table drawer, she pulls a plastic bag containing a pipe and a couple of pill bottles. One holds marijuana, the other hashish. She scrapes tiny pieces off the hashish stone with a double-edged razor blade, then goes through the ritual of combining the grass with the hashish and stuffing the mixture into the pipe. She lights the pipe, inhales, and keeps the concoction in her lungs for an eternity. She doesn't offer the pipe to me.

"I'm sorry, I don't have that much," she says. "It's expensive. My boy friend got the stuff in Cannes."

Would smoking distract her from talking about the Soli decision?

"Why do you think I'm doing it? It helps me.

"Let's see. So we got into the room and we all knew it was a grave affair. Everyone would say a little something. Some jurors were strong, some weak, but nobody tried to push. I found that the women were basically softer than the men. Donna DePaul's clothes, for instance, were discussed at length. Some women were impressed with how she dressed. One woman said that Donna's blouse had never been worn before."

Did Knight's homosexuality come up?

"Not much. Tinari was trying to push it, but we didn't talk about it much in deliberation. Knight's wealth did, though. Some jurors were in awe of it."

The thrust of the discussion had to do with the conspiracy charge. All the jurors agreed that Soli was involved from the start. Not enough evidence was presented to prove that Melendez killed Knight in an action completely isolated from the break-in. They deliberated for six hours, then broke to eat.

"The tension was too high," she says. "I wasn't able to touch my food."

Of course, they finally found Soli guilty and presented their decision to Judge Williams. "Then we returned to the jury room after Tinari made us each say he was guilty. Well, when we got back, most of us were weeping. The men were shaking. Everyone was involved. You get crazy. It wasn't a cool, cool thing.''

She takes a couple of more tokes from the pipe. The smoke that fills the room is getting me high. She asks me to read back what I have written. I do. She reminds herself that she hasn't told me what happened after they found Soli guilty. "We had to decide on his sentence. He came pretty close to getting it. You don't know how close we were to giving him the chair.''

How close?

"Only three votes prevented him from getting it.''

I ask if her vote was one.

"Yes. I was one of them.''

Later, much later, I tell this to Soli. He is in the Camden County Jail, the same jail where I visited Joe Paolucci. A glass partition separates us.

"They might as well have given me the death penalty,'' he says. "It's the same thing, being in jail the rest of your life.''

Getting to visit him has not been easy. At first, Nino Tinari refused to allow me near his client. Then Soli dropped Tinari. He hired another lawyer to represent him on the Melendez charge.

At one point, Soli complained to correctional officers that his life was in jeopardy: he had received death threats from fellow inmates. Consequently, he was transferred to the Correctional Institute at Dallas, Pennsylvania, and was later transferred to the jail in Camden.

Soli's new attorney agreed to get us together, but the warden at Camden County maintained that extensive repair work was being done within the jail and vetoed my seeing him.

The status of the visit became an obsession with Soli. We talked on the phone several times. He tried pulling strings: he spoke to a caseworker, who couldn't help.

Meanwhile, Soli got into a scrape. After beating up a cellmate, he aired his grievances to the warden, and one complaint was that the system wouldn't allow him visitors other than his attorney and immediate family. About a week after that, the visit was arranged.

Unlike my last excursion into Camden territory, there is no chance of physical contact because we are literally in two separate rooms, Soli and me. And there is shock, genuine shock, at the sight of him. He wears a dirty orange jump suit. He's grown stouter. Bags have accumulated under his eyes. Any semblance of the bon vivant is gone. In its place is a short, unattractive, middle-aged man with stubby fingers, a pencil-thin moustache, and a kindly gruff manner. He reminds me of the men who played blackjack on Brooklyn stoops during summer heat waves when I was a kid.

Around us, jail doors clang open and shut, but no guard is posted in the chamber where Sal sits, leaning forward in a stiff wooden chair. The room is bereft of other furniture. The walls are cream-colored and a fluorescent light shines down on the concrete floor.

"How are they treating you, Sal? Okay?"

"No," he answers. "Believe me, it's terrible. I've never seen a jail like this in my life. The worst prison I've ever been to."

I refrain from smiling. Does one judge the worst prison the same way one judges the worst hotel?

"It would have been better," he says, "if you visited me in Huntington. The man there is the greatest warden. Here, they've got me on an assault and battery charge and attempted escape, as well as everything else. I tried to get out and got as far as the gate, then they caught me."

"Do you mind talking about what happened after the trial?"

"No. Because I feel I got a bum deal. I didn't kill John Knight. There's no doubt in nobody's mind. I'm sure of that. Why I'm here is everybody's fault. As far as I'm concerned, they were all bought off."

"What proof do you have? Who would have bought them?"

"The Knight family. To keep everything quieted down, which it did. Nothing came out in the trials about Knight's life. If I had taken the stand, it would have been an altogether different story. They said it was a grudge thing—I didn't even know the man. December 7 was the first time I saw John Knight in my life."

"Fitzpatrick said it was a grudge thing between Knight and Melendez."

"Yeah. But not the way they brought it out in the trial. If you recall, Fitzpatrick said, 'The man had a grudge against him,' meaning me against Knight. That's not true at all. Because I said to Melendez in the apartment when I saw him kicking Knight—I said, 'Why are you doing that to that man? He's tied up. He's not doing nothing.' There's no way in the world that this man, John Knight, should have been dead. I understand that part. But I don't see where I should take all the weight because I didn't know nothing about the man getting killed. The man was alive when I left there. That's why I got the hell out. Because things were getting out of hand, with Melendez stalking up and down the apartment. That's all he was doing. He had on this scuba diving outfit with the knives on the side and a scuba diving gun."

"Was Knight still alive when Melendez was kicking him?"

"He was still alive when I left there. Even Mrs. McKinnon knows that. Felix kept on running back to the other room, turning on the record player, running back again, turning the record player up again, turning the phonograph down, then running back again. But they couldn't convict Melendez because he's dead, so naturally they had to convict somebody. The most I should have been found guilty of is attempted burglary. The only thing I took was a gold chain out of there. Stevie Maleno took nothing. Felix is the only one who took anything—the stuff they found in Paolucci's house. Oh, yeah . . . I took a little over $190 in cash. We were looking for drugs."

"You don't think that Stevie Maleno had anything to do with Knight's death?"

"I doubt that very much. There's no way. He punched the man a couple of times. But not like what Felix was doing. Everytime I went into the other room, Felix was saying, 'You shouldn't have done that to me, John,' and I'd catch him kicking John. In fact, I caught Felix and I hit him on the head with the rifle. That's when I grabbed him and said, 'Why are you doing that to that man, Felix? Why are you doing that?' He said, 'Because he did something to me. He did something.' I wasn't paying no attention then, you know, but I cracked Melendez across the head with the rifle."

"Did you know Felix was gay?"

"No. I had no idea."

"But now you know for a fact."

"Oh, yeah. Even his roommate, Joe Paolucci, he even said that afterward. Felix admitted to me right in a Jersey motel room, that him and John had things going together. Felix used to go up to John's place all the time."

"Do you think Felix did it because he was in love with Knight?"

"That's the only thing I can think of. Even when Felix was on the phone talking to Knight, he told him,

'John, please give me another chance, let me come over and talk to you.' When he was knocking at Knight's apartment door, even, he was saying, 'John, please open the door. Give me another chance. Please. I love you. John.' ''

Soli's voice is low as he recounts this part. He places his little hands together in a pleading gesture and his eyes look heavenward. It's not Little Eva. But it's not acting, either. I don't know what it is.

"Did Felix know that John had visitors?"

"Yeah. He did know that. I think he was jealous, that's what I think."

I take a deep breath and ask Soli if he himself ever had any sexual experiences with men. He claims he never did. "I know a lot of gays," he admits, "but I never had nothing to do with them. They were friends of mine, that's all. That's as far as it went."

"You never played them for money?"

"Nah. Anybody who knows me can tell you that. You can ask anybody in Philadelphia who knows me. I have a lot of friends that are gay people. That's what I'm saying. They're friends of mine. That's the understanding we have together. We're friends. That's as far as it goes."

Thinking of Joe Paolucci "playing the queers," I ask Sal if he's ever protected gay men from getting beat up?

"I never had the opportunity to see anything like this happen. But the gay people I associate with are from downtown and Center City. Most of the ones I know were born and raised with me. Friends of mine who turned gay after a certain age."

"So there wasn't a vengeance theme between you and Knight?"

"What?" he exclaims. "No way in the world. See, I don't have no malice in my heart for people like that. I like all people. As long as they're all right with me. To each his own. Whatever somebody wants to be—that's their prerogative.''

He sounds just like a pamphlet from the National Gay Task Force. Can he explain why Mrs. McKinnon might have thought he was gay?

''Yeah. Because I protected her. Stevie wanted to rape her. Right? And I turned around and gave her the sheet to put around her body. Maybe that's why.''

I contradict him and suggest that maybe it's because he found a dildo in Knight's apartment and was holding it in his grasp and Mrs. McKinnon was getting ideas, albeit the wrong ones.

''I found a whole bagful of apparatus. Dildoes was just one of the apparatus.''

''What were the other apparatus?''

''There was a whole big traveling bag of all sexual toys. I gave Mrs. McKinnon a dildo and asked her, 'What do you use these for? Don't your husband satisfy you?' She didn't answer. She was trying to use psychology, you know, to try to calm everybody down.''

''Did Mrs. McKinnon talk with Felix anywhere along the line?''

''She said she sat and talked with him for quite a while, after we left.''

''Do you think John was dead at the time that she was talking to Felix?''

''I don't believe so. Because at the trial, she said Felix kept running in and out of the room where she was. I left her tied real light. I told her that I wasn't going to tie her tight, just so she could later get out of there. She wasn't under the couch, by the way, like they said. She could have seen right into the other room. She was on top of the pillows. I put the pillows there because I didn't want her just laying on the floor.''

"What about the doctor? Did he really sleep through the whole mess?"

"I don't believe he was sleeping. There's no way in the world he could have been sleeping because the janitor came up and Felix told him that he and John were practicing karate, so you can imagine how much noise was being made."

Apparently not enough noise to get the McKinnons up immediately. Sal claims that he was in the apartment for perhaps half an hour before he discovered them in the guest room. Were the McKinnons in the same bed?

"Yeah. It was like a double bed. I shook the doctor, and all. His wife said, 'Please leave him alone. He's drunk. He fell out from drinking.' "

"And he didn't awaken?"

"No. He didn't move an inch. That's why I know that he was playing possum. There's no doubt in my mind. If the man wanted to tell exactly what went down in that apartment, he could probably tell everything that went on there. But he didn't move from that room once. And I didn't touch him—not a hand was laid on him. All I did was shake him.

"That's why I had to keep running back and forth, you understand. Every time I left the room where the doctor was, I'd catch Melendez acting crazy to Knight. Then I had to run back to the other room to see if the doctor was still there. Back and forth, back and forth. You know what I mean?"

"Was Knight screaming?"

"That's what I heard. I heard John screaming. Every time I walked in that room, he was screaming. Felix kept saying, 'John, you shouldn't have did that to me, John.' That's all he kept saying. He was wired out, you understand. From the speed. And I guess all his emotions came out. And I was wired out, too."

A weird thing happens. Soli's voice cracks. He tries to hold back a sob. And I remember Marilyn Schaeffer explaining the character of the Philadelphia Italian while we were waiting for the jury's verdict. She said that she would have been shocked had Soli's family not appeared in court every day. She said the Italian community are clannish and supportive of each other and are given to outbursts. I silently pray I'm not about to witness another Soli family outburst, though I feel great compassion for Sal—sorrow, in fact. I really believe that he's a punk who got caught in an out-of-control situation, but I withhold telling him what I think, and ask him if he thinks that Knight was alive when he and Stevie left his apartment.

"He was still alive then. The only thing he had was a few marks on his face."

"How are you sure he was alive?"

"He was moving, making motions."

"But he wasn't able to talk. Right? He was gagged. Right?"

"Yeah," Sal replies, "but his eyes were open. He was motioning and moving around. Even Mrs. McKinnon saw him alive. Believe me, I went there with different intentions. The man was supposed to have a lot of drugs. If I was straight, I would have known better than to stay there. But I was high. I should have used my sense."

In a way, it's difficult to comprehend Sal using his sense, or, for that matter, to believe everything he's saying. This is no George Washington. This is not a pillar of the community. Look at his record. He was first arrested in March 1957 on a delinquency charge and since been arrested fifty-two times before the Knight case.

Perhaps there is something fishy in this game of confess that Sal is playing with me. Certainly, there are gaps in his story. But a man with nothing to lose is more likely to tell the truth than a man with everything to lose. And now Sal has nothing, except his life, which he doesn't seem to hold in high esteem.

I ask him if he's bumped into Joe Paolucci in Camden, and he replies that they've transferred Joe to another jail. He hasn't seen Stevie Maleno, either. Not since the last time, when Stevie visited the motel in Jersey with his wife. The authorities deliberately keep them in different penitentiaries. A month after Sal's Philadelphia trial, Stevie pleaded guilty to both murders and is serving two consecutive life sentences.

"How about Linda and Donna?"

"I saw Linda when they came to Huntington to extradite me back here. Donna's at a federal prison in Lexington, Kentucky, on a drug charge."

"Linda says you were fucking with her when you fled from Jersey to Florida."

"Well, I was fucking with both of them. Linda and Donna."

"And Donna got jealous?"

"I imagine. Then Linda got scared. I don't blame her for turning me in. I was balling them both at the same time. It doesn't make no difference, because neither one of them really meant nothing to me.

"Mr. Bell," he says. "I know you're a writer, but why are you interested in all this? Did you know John Knight?"

I tell Sal that I feel that I knew John, but I had never met him.

"You seem so interested, and I don't think you're that interested in me."

I assure Sal that I am.

A prison guard calls. The session is ended. Sal asks me to phone him if I need anything else. He says he's sure to beat the Melendez murder rap in Jersey. "But let me explain to you," he adds, just before he's led back to his cell. "I don't feel nothing about Melendez being dead. As far as I'm concerned, he deserved to die. But Knight—there was no reason in the world why that man should be dead. No reason at all."

Early March. Three hours by bus from Altanta. No one on the suburban street. Rain falls on my head as I approach the sprawling building, its architecture half Tara, half White House.

Columbus High School, 1925, reads the cornerstone, but the administrator who leads me to the locked cabinet in the library claims the school was built much earlier. She pulls a copy of the 1960 yearbook from the bottom shelf. I take it to a table, away from the main room where the senior class is viewing a Bill Cosby TV show on tolerance. I sit, and leaf through the book.

Tradition: the carrying on of tradition, underscored and emphasized, page after page.

Page 1: A quote from "Song of the Chattahoochee" by Sidney Lanier.

> Downward the voices of Duty call—
> Downward, to toil and be mixed with the main,
> The dry fields burn, and the mills are to turn
> And a myriad flowers mortally yearn . . .

A headline on the sports page: "Students' moods are like the river—turbulent, then calm." Next to the caption a photograph of the winning football team. Fourteen-year-old Johnny Knight, front row, kneeling.

Page 17: Two dozen tiny photo-booth face shots. Johnny Knight and his classmates. Johnny's forehead is wide, his hair neatly combed and parted, his eyes two tiny darts squinting, pug nose, firm jaw, white shirt, tie. Not easily distinguishable from any of the other healthy young men in the junior class. Except this young man's mouth is crooked in a mocking smile.

I look at the picture, mesmerized, chilled, knowing how the flower died, staring at the seed.

I tear the page from the book. And leave.

On February 3, 1978, Salvatore Soli is found guilty of the murder of Felix Melendez, and is sentenced, once again, to life imprisonment.

ABOUT THE AUTHOR

Arthur Bell is a staff writer and columnist for
The Village Voice. His work has also appeared in
Esquire, The New York Times, Playboy, and
Cosmopolitan and has covered a wide range of
subjects—from murders, marches, movie stars,
and bank robberies to asexuality, homosexuality,
politics, riots, and weddings. He was born in
Brooklyn, N.Y., lives in Manhattan, and is the
author of *Dancing the Gay Lib Blues*, published
in 1971.

New Bestsellers from Berkley
The best in paperback reading

___ **BY THE RIVERS OF BABYLON**   04431-9—$2.75
Nelson De Mille

___ **THE LAST CONVERTIBLE**   04034-8—$2.50
Anton Myrer

___ **LEAH'S JOURNEY**   04430-0—$2.50
Gloria Goldreich

___ **THE LEGACY**   04183-2—$2.25
John Coyne, based on a story by Jimmy Sangster

___ **MOMMIE DEAREST**   04444-0—$2.75
Christina Crawford

___ **NO BED OF ROSES**   04241-3—$2.50
Joan Fontaine

___ **NURSE**   04220-0—$2.50
Peggy Anderson

___ **PURSUIT**   04258-8—$2.50
Robert L. Fish

___ **THE TANGENT FACTOR**   04120-4—$2.25
Lawrence Sanders

___ **A TIME FOR TRUTH**   04185-9—$2.50
William E. Simon

1

The Best of Berkley's Nonfiction